"Jesus Christ is the same yesterday and today and forever." —Hebrews 13:8

JESUS
IS WITH US

The Treasure of Jesus' Presence in Your Life

A 12-Session Bible Study on God's Plan for Your Life

Published by Gospel Light
Ventura, California, U.S.A.
www.gospellight.com
Printed in the U.S.A.

All Scripture quotations, unless otherwise indicated, are taken from the *Holy Bible, New International Version®*. Copyright © 1973, 1978, 1984 by International Bible Society. Used by permission of Zondervan Publishing House. All rights reserved. Other version used is *KJV—King James Version*. Authorized King James Version.

© 2013 Gospel Light.
All rights reserved.

Information in the "Old West Characters" sidebars taken from Wikipedia.org.
All photos used are in the public domain.

Rights for publishing this book outside the U.S.A. or in non-English languages are administered by Gospel Light Worldwide, an international not-for-profit ministry. For additional information, please visit www.glww.org, email info@glww.org, or write to Gospel Light Worldwide, 1957 Eastman Avenue, Ventura, CA 93003, U.S.A.

To order copies of this book and other Gospel Light products in bulk quantities, please contact us at 1-800-446-7735.

CONTENTS

Introduction: Our Western Heritage and the Bible 5

Session 1: **Ultimate Plan** 13
Exodus 1–2:10

Session 2: **Ultimate Power** 23
Exodus 3–4

Session 3: **Ultimate Rescue** 33
Exodus 5–12

Session 4: **Ultimate Trust** 43
Exodus 16–17:7

Session 5: **Ultimate Love** 53
Exodus 19–20.21, 24.12, 23.10–22

Session 6: **Ultimate Courage** 63
Genesis 37; 39

Session 7: **Ultimate Moral Compass** 73
Genesis 40–41

Session 8: **Ultimate Abundance** 83
Genesis 42–47; 50:15–21

Session 9: **Ultimate Redemption** 93
Psalms 66; 105:12–41

Session 10: **Ultimate Allegiance** 103
Deuteronomy 4

Session 11: **Ultimate Legacy** 113
Deuteronomy 6

Session 12: **Ultimate Sustenance** 123
Deuteronomy 8; 28

Appendix A: Leading a Bible Study 133

Appendix B: Joining God's Family 137

INTRODUCTION

OUR WESTERN HERITAGE AND THE BIBLE

He waters the mountains from his upper chambers; the earth is satisfied by the fruit of his work. He makes grass grow for the cattle, and plants for man to cultivate—bringing forth food from the earth.

PSALM 104:13-14

The Old West—or its more "colorful" name, the Wild West—has left an indelible imprint on the American psyche: Kids play cowboys and Indians; rodeos feature cowboys roping steers and riding bucking broncos; movie Westerns feed our imaginations with vivid depictions of cowboys, outlaws, Texas Rangers, Pony Express riders and Native Americans; and country music fills the airwaves with the twang of guitars and down-home lyrics.

OUR INHERITANCE FROM THE OLD WEST

As adults, we relate to the story of the Old West on many levels. For one thing, there was a change in fashion. When they took to the Old West, men discarded powdered wigs and silk stockings, put on some tougher clothes and grew some hair. Women packed away their fancy dresses and donned simpler clothing. These changes reflected a shift in orientation from an eastward look toward the classical and refined traditions of Europe to a westward look focused on a vast, untamed frontier requiring an optimistic, can-do spirit. The pioneers of the American frontier were not afraid of hard work and taking a pragmatic approach to life; in fact, both were necessary for their survival.

On another level, we can relate to the story of the Old West because it was a time when the fledgling nation was rapidly expanding to become the country we live in today. Overnight, the Louisiana Purchase of 1803 doubled the territory of the United States. Those in power wondered just what it was that we had taken on. New ways of thinking and of doing things were needed. Intrepid explorers were needed—men who could make accurate maps and keep meticulous records—and then came trappers, scouts and traders; loggers, miners and ranchers appeared; figures like Lewis and Clark, Daniel Boone and the defenders of the Alamo became the stuff of legend, as did lawmen like Wyatt Earp and outlaws like Jesse James. Ideas like Manifest Destiny came into play, and projects like the Transcontinental Railroad took shape. The vast land of this country attracted all sorts of people and promised to be either the answer to prayers or the reason to start praying. The very size of the land seemed to offer unlimited possibilities—an attraction that holds true even today.

Out of our quick westward expansion came another level on which we can relate: our attitude toward nature. To lay claim to the land, the explorers, mountain men, traders, soldiers, cowboys, ranchers and miners lived most of their lives outdoors, enduring whatever nature might throw at them. Nature was to be respected. This meant learning to appreciate and even at times accommodate nature. Eventually, nature came to be valued in and of itself, rather than just in terms of its monetary worth or what it could produce. This attitude led to a movement to set aside portions of land in this country and create state and national parks.

On the other side of the nature "coin," however, is the fact that many of those traders, soldiers, cowboys, ranchers and miners who lived on the land also had the need to subjugate the land. This attitude necessitated clearing the land of trees, of animals and of people, be they Native Americans, Spaniards or Mexicans. Civilization and progress were at the forefront—and so was the rise of racist attitudes and feelings of cultural superiority.

Whereas there is much that is beautiful and mutually enriching about our Western heritage, care must be taken to not overly simplify or romanticize our past.

THE PERIL OF NOSTALGIA

From a biblical and moral perspective, our Western heritage is not an unmixed blessing. Yes, there is much to admire in it. But it is a human project, and as a human project it is messy. As humans, we seek to justify our existence; if we are in a position of privilege, power or dominance, we tend to romanticize the past, forgetting, downplaying or whitewashing the wrongs our ancestors have done. In our history, there is much to applaud, but there is also much at which to cringe.

As we do with our history, so too we do with many of our heroes: We tend to lionize our heroes, magnifying their virtues and forgetting their faults. The Bible doesn't do this with its heroes. The Bible takes its heroes down a few pegs, enabling us to see ourselves in their vain, selfish, self-serving and often self-defeating characters. The only biblical hero that this doesn't happen to is Jesus, and there are important reasons for that.

THE "OLD WEST" IN THE BIBLE

In some respects, the biblical story is similar to the story of the Old West, especially if we think of the magnificent but harsh Southwest. In the book of Exodus, an agrarian people living in a highly civilized culture (Egypt) were forced into slavery, escaped and then had to fend for themselves in an arid, inhospitable wilderness before they entered the Promised Land. In the Old West, people who lived in or near a highly civilized culture (cities in the East) "escaped" from city life and had to fend for themselves in an arid, inhospitable wilderness before they reached their "Promised Land" (prosperity).

THE CREATOR OF THE OLD WEST (AND EVERYTHING ELSE)

Whether the Old West being discussed is that of the Bible or of America, God has always been there. In the Bible, God is always understood as the Creator (see Genesis 1:1; Psalm 24:1). God is the author of everything and all life (see Genesis 1–2). And several psalms express amazement at all that God has done as Creator (see, for example, Psalms 8; 19; 139).

And when we take the whole testimony of the Bible that says God is the Creator, we bump square into the fact that the pre-incarnate Christ was with God in the beginning:

In the beginning was the Word, and the Word was with God, and the Word was God. He was with God in the beginning. Through him all things were made; without him nothing was made that has been made (John 1:1-3).

He [Jesus] is the image of the invisible God, the firstborn over all creation. For by him all things were created: things in heaven and on earth, visible and invisible, whether thrones or powers or rulers or authorities; all things were created by him and for him. He is before all things, and in him all things hold together (Colossians 1:15-17).

The connection between God and Jesus is first made in Genesis 1:1-3, where God (Hebrew *elohim*), the Spirit of God (Hebrew *ruach*, breath or spirit), and the Word of God (Hebrew *amar*, to speak) are all involved in the Creation. We also see this connection made in Proverbs 8:22-31, in which personified Wisdom raises her voice and talks about how she was involved in every aspect of Creation; and in the apostle Paul's first letter to the Corinthians, in which he talks about Christ as "the power of God and the wisdom of God" (1 Corinthians 1:24).

In this direct linking of God the Father's role in Creation, the Son of God and His role in Creation, and the Holy Spirit's role in Creation, we have the foundational truth that is the main theme of this study: "Jesus Christ is the same yesterday and today and forever" (Hebrews 13:8). Jesus was in the beginning, is now with us and will be forever with His disciples.

Psalm 104 is a summary of God's Creation, but the psalmist also points out that God maintains His Creation:

He waters the mountains from his upper chambers; the earth is satisfied by the fruit of his work. He makes grass grow for the cattle, and plants for man to cultivate—bringing forth food from the earth (verses 13-14).

These all [all living things] look to you [God] to give them their food at the proper time. When you give it to them, they gather it up; when you open your hand, they are satisfied with good things. When you hide your face, they are terrified; when you take away their breath, they die and return to the dust. When you send

INTRODUCTION: OUR WESTERN HERITAGE AND THE BIBLE

your Spirit, they are created, and you renew the face of the earth (verses 27-30).

It is clear that God provides for all of life, including us. And not only is God's power to provide for us unlimited, but it also has been at work in us from the beginning. Jesus' work in our lives did not start only at salvation, when we started believing in Him. It goes way back to the dawn of Creation and will continue through all eternity. This is why we don't just tip our hat to Jesus; we worship Him.

DESCRIPTION OF THE COURSE

Each of the 12 sessions in this study will help you discover the treasure of Jesus' enduring presence with us. Although this study can be used as an adult component of Gospel Light's 2013 Vacation Bible School program *SonWest Roundup* (the first five sessions mimic the five sessions of the children's Vacation Bible School), it can also be used as a 12-week stand-alone study.

	VBS Session	Theme/Lesson Focus	Bible Story/Reference
1	Ultimate PLAN	God cared about the Israelites and sent Moses to help them. God sent Jesus because He cares about us.	God cared about His people when they were in trouble and sent Moses (Exodus 1–2:10).
2	Ultimate POWER	God used His power to help Moses. Jesus' power is big enough to help us—no matter what.	God proved His power to Moses at the burning bush (Exodus 3–4).
3	Ultimate RESCUE	God saved the Israelites from slavery in Egypt. Jesus' death and resurrection can save us from sin and give us eternal life.	God rescued His people at Passover (Exodus 5–12).

	VBS Session	Theme/Lesson Focus	Bible Story/Reference
4	Ultimate TRUST	The Israelites could trust God to provide for them. We can trust Jesus to take care of us every day.	God met the needs of His people in the desert by giving them food and water (Exodus 16–17:7).
5	Ultimate LOVE	God gave commands for the Israelites to follow. Jesus' new command is to follow Him and love others.	On Mount Sinai, God gave Moses the Ten Commandments so that His people knew how to love and obey Him (Exodus 19–20:21; 24:12; 25:10-22).

	12-Week Session	Theme/Lesson Focus	Bible Story/Reference
6	Ultimate Courage	God was with Joseph and saw him through every trouble that he faced. Jesus is with us to guide us through every challenge that we face.	God gave Joseph dreams of his future and challenges to overcome (Genesis 37; 39).
7	Ultimate Moral Compass	Joseph followed God's moral compass, and God delivered him from prison to a palace. Jesus is the model for our moral compass, and He delivers us from sin to eternal life.	God delivered Joseph from the prison and helped him interpret the king's dreams (Genesis 40–41).
8	Ultimate Abundance	God provided abundantly for Joseph and enabled him to be a blessing to others. Jesus provided abundantly for us and wants us to be a blessing to others.	Joseph's family went to Egypt, and Joseph forgave them (Genesis 42–47; 50:15-21).

Introduction: Our Western Heritage and the Bible

	12-Week Session	Theme/Lesson Focus	Bible Story/Reference
9	Ultimate Redemption	God revealed His will and intentions in the Old Testament. Jesus, revealed in the New Testament, fulfilled God's will and intention to redeem us.	God saved His people in the past, and for that He should be praised (Psalms 66; 105:12-41).
10	Ultimate Allegiance	God protected His Chosen People and wanted them to obey only Him. Jesus will always protect those who follow Him and obey Him.	Moses reminded the Israelites of what God had done for them and why they should obey God (Deuteronomy 4).
11	Ultimate Legacy	God told parents to teach their children to love and obey Him. Jesus will help every generation to love and obey Him.	Moses directed the Israelites to love God with all their hearts, souls and strength and to teach their children to do the same (Deuteronomy 6).
12	Ultimate Sustenance	God tested and humbled the Israelites to teach them to depend on Him alone. Jesus shows us our need to humble ourselves and rely only on Him.	Moses reminded the Israelites of why they could depend on God and told them about the blessings of obedience and the curses of disobedience (Deuteronomy 8; 28).

SESSION ONE

ULTIMATE PLAN

Exodus 1–2:10

SESSION FOCUS

God cared about the Israelites and sent Moses to help them. God sent Jesus to be our mighty deliverer because He cares about us.

KEY VERSE

For God so loved the world that he gave his one and only Son, that whoever believes in him shall not perish but have eternal life.

JOHN 3:16

SESSION AT A GLANCE

Section	60 Min.	90 Min.	What You Will Do
Getting started	10	15	Pray and worship
Main points of the chapter	25	35	Discuss the lonesome stranger motif in the Bible
Application and discussion	15	25	Discuss personal application questions
Looking ahead	5	5	Prepare for next week
Wrapping up	5	10	Close with prayer or song

The United States of America is a young, muscular and brash country. We began with 13 separate colonies clustered on the East Coast. Once established as an independent nation, we started pushing ever and inexorably westward. We leapfrogged the Great Lakes, scaled the Appalachian Mountains, worked our way up great river valleys, made our way across the Deep South, pioneered the Great Plains, and stretched ourselves to the Pacific Ocean.

From our founding, we grew at a breakneck pace. Our plan eventually came to be known as Manifest Destiny, the belief that the expansion of the United States across the continent was inevitable. As we explored the wild, wide-open American landscape, we asserted ourselves over Native American, British, French, Spanish, Russian and Mexican claims and interests. We believed that we had the God-given right and duty to bring our kind of civilization to the wilderness and expand our nation from sea to shining sea.

Through it all, the complex westward movement and the pioneering spirit that drove it have became deeply ingrained in our collective American consciousness.

THE WESTERN IN FICTION

Our American experience of westward expansion—"taming" the wilderness, overcoming natural as well as man-made threats to our survival—eventually gave rise to the Western, a category found in a variety of arts, including literature, painting and film, which typically tells stories about the Old West. Normally, the setting of a Western is somewhere in the relatively unsettled American West sometime between 1860 and 1900. The mode of transportation is usually limited to horses and/or stagecoaches. Eastern towns and cities, supposed guardians of civilization and law, are far, far away. The frontier West is "wild" and lawless. What towns there are, are gritty little affairs, and each one is usually "a dirty little village in the middle of nowhere. Nothing that happens [in it] is really important."[1]

In a typical Western plot, a town is terrorized and paralyzed by a gang of outlaws. If the town has a sheriff, he is weak and ineffectual. The people cannot save themselves from the outlaws' threats and violence. Then, into the town rides a lonesome stranger with understated but undeniable skills with a gun. The stranger is persuaded—by the offer of money, the love of a woman or his own code of honor—to come to the defense of the town. The stranger meets violence with violence and vanquishes the outlaws. At the end of the story, the stranger rides off into the sunset, often with the woman he loves.

THE WESTERN IN THE BIBLE

The similarities between the typical Western plot and one of the great storylines in the Old Testament is pretty clear. The book of Exodus opens with the Egyptians perpetrating an outrageous injustice against a minority community, the Hebrews, or Israelites: The Israelites were forced into slave labor to build the Egyptians cities of Pithom and Rameses.

But the Egyptians were worried: The Israelites had an exceedingly high birth rate. If the Israelites kept reproducing like they had been, the Egyptians figured that they would overrun the country. So the king of Egypt commanded the Israelite midwives to kill the male children immediately after they were born. The midwives resisted his immoral order, claiming that unlike Egyptian women, the Israelite women gave birth so quickly that the Israelite midwives could not help them have their babies. Even so, as a community, the Israelites were in a terrible fix from which they were unable to extricate themselves.

In Exodus 2 (please read the entire chapter, not just the first 10 verses), the Bible says something very interesting, something we really need to sit up and pay attention to:

> The Israelites groaned in their slavery and cried out, and their cry for help because of their slavery went up to God. God heard their groaning and he remembered his covenant with Abraham, with Isaac and with Jacob. So God looked on the Israelites and was concerned about them (Exodus 2:23-25).

There are four things to note in this passage. First, the Israelites were really hurting, and they loudly and repeatedly begged for release from their slavery. (If you're in a bad situation, it's not wrong to want to change your situation, and it's never a bad idea to go to your knees and ask God to change things.)

Second, even though the Israelites had been suffering for a long time, God heard their prayers. It might have seemed to them that their prayers were hitting a bronze ceiling; but somehow those prayers *were* getting through.

Third, God had not forgotten His promises to Abraham, Isaac and Jacob—the forefathers of the Israelites. Now that God "remembered" His promise doesn't mean that God had had amnesia for a while. This metaphorical language means that it may have seemed as if God might have forgotten about the Israelites, because their circumstances were so horrific. But God hadn't forgotten. He was just getting things ready to make a big change in their circumstances. God doesn't make pie-in-the-sky promises. He was about to act decisively in their social, historical, real-life, this-world, concrete situation. God knows when is the best time to act. And He always has a plan in mind.

Fourth, God was moved with compassion for the Israelites. God cared deeply for His Chosen People. God never abandons those who believe in Him; and His responsiveness reflects His love and supreme control over everything—and it reveals a part of His plan.

THE MOTIF OF THE LONESOME STRANGER

In Westerns, the hero is often a misfit, a loner, somebody with a past that's best left alone. He's a drifter, without a wife or home, moving from place to place, never putting down roots. After he sets things right, he moves on. Usually he can't be tied down or thoroughly domesticated.

In Exodus 2, we can see that in some significant ways, Moses fit that description. Although born an Israelite, early on he was separated from his people. For 40 years he lived among the Egyptians, but after he killed an overseer who was beating a worker, he had to flee to the desert. In the desert, he aligned himself for the next 40 years with the Midianites, a nomadic people, and took a wife. Then one day in the desert, Moses noticed a burning bush and had an amazing, miraculous encounter with the God

OLD WEST CHARACTERS
DANIEL BOONE (1734–1820)

Daniel Boone was a pioneer, explorer and frontiersman whose numerous exploits made him one of the first folk heroes in the United States. He is most renown for his exploration and settlement of what is now the state of Kentucky. In 1778, Boone was captured by Shawnee warriors, who, after allowing him to spend some time among them, adopted him into their tribe. He served as a militia officer during the Revolutionary War and served three terms in the Virginia General Assembly. Boone became a "legend in his own lifetime" after a book recounting his adventures was first published in 1784.

Photo: Painting by John James Audubon (1785-1851). Public domain.

of the Israelites (see Exodus 3). God told him that he (Moses) would lead the Israelites out of slavery in Egypt.

Moses both fulfilled and broke the lonesome stranger mold. He fulfilled it—and his destiny—by being God's means to end the violent oppression of His people and freeing them. But Moses broke the mold by maintaining his family ties and forming a covenant community bound by laws (think the Ten Commandments). He also broke the mold by not personally being a "gunslinger" but by trusting God to fight the really big fights for him. At the end of his life, Moses didn't exactly ride off into the sunset, but he did make a memorable exit (see Deuteronomy 34).

THE TRUE DISTRESS OF THE COMMUNITY

In the typical storyline of a Western, the townspeople are powerless to help themselves, as mentioned previously. If anyone in the town has tried to right the wrongs done in the town or to it, that person has been killed. The community is distressed, downcast and adrift, without a plan to right the situation. The community wants to be saved but has no idea how to go about doing that. What they need is a larger-than-life hero.

Similarly, in the Bible, God's people were distressed, downcast and spiritually adrift. Deceived by the devil and oppressed by their own sins and the devil himself, they were unable to make their situation right. They knew they needed help but had no plan to actually change the situation. They needed a larger-than-life hero. The community needed a savior to rescue it, because "the wages of sin is death" (Romans 6:23).

Fortunately, God never leaves us to fend for ourselves. From the very beginning, He had a plan to meet our need.

THE RESCUE BY THE LONESOME STRANGER NAMED JESUS

In the Western's storyline, when the community seems to be on its last legs before succumbing to final defeat and an end to everything they've known and loved, the larger-than-life hero rides into town. Unassuming but having a commanding presence, the lonesome stranger regards the town, sees what needs doing and does it. Asking nothing for himself (though he is often rewarded by the love of a good woman), he does what he does because he knows that it's the right thing to do.

Long after God used Moses as a lonesome stranger to rescue His Chosen People from oppression in Egypt, at a time when the human community had gone through kings and prophets and captivities and returns, at a time when they were in danger of finally succumbing to their own sinful natures, God fulfilled His plan to send another lonesome stranger to the people to rescue them—Jesus!

Like Moses, Jesus both fulfilled and broke the lonesome stranger mold. He fulfilled the mold in that He certainly was a lonesome stranger. Yes, He gained disciples, but Jesus was unlike any other human. First off, what made Jesus particularly strange was the fact that as eternal Son of God, He took on flesh and became one of us (see John 1:1-3,14)! What could be stranger, or lonelier, than that!

And although we know that Jesus was born in Bethlehem and grew up in Nazareth, after Jesus' twelfth year, we lose sight of him for 18 years. We aren't told again what He was doing until He is baptized by John. He is something of a mysterious character to us. He didn't marry. He didn't settle down. He couldn't be pigeonholed or controlled. He didn't quite fit in with other people; unlike the rest of us, He perfectly followed His moral compass.

Yet it was this outsider, who Himself was without sin, who was the only One who was able to free us from the penalty and power of our sins. He defeated the cruel and lawless one (Satan) who oppresses the community of humankind.

But in a strange twist to the story, Jesus dealt a death-blow to the violent oppressor's power by giving up His own life for our sakes. Jesus fulfilled God's plan that His Son's sacrifice would pay the price for our sins, shattering the power of the devil over us. In another twist, this lonesome stranger Jesus returned from the dead, left His Spirit with us and, while not exactly "riding off into the sunset," went back to the Father to await the culmination of all things (see Acts 1:11).

Jesus also broke the lonesome stranger mold by not just rescuing the human community that existed during His time, but by also rescuing all future generations of humankind. In God's great wisdom, Jesus' fulfillment of His plan purchased our salvation: "For God so loved the world that he gave his one and only Son, that whoever believes in him shall not perish but have eternal life" (John 3:16).

REFLECTION QUESTIONS

Why do you think that Westerns are deeply ingrained in American culture and have continued to be a favorite genre in books and movies?

Where have you seen the Old West depicted, and how accurate do you think the portrayals have been?

How is the storyline of Exodus 1–2 similar to a typical Western?

How is it different?

Although it is unlikely that you will ever be enslaved like the Israelites were in Egypt, you may have felt (or feel) oppressed by problems or troubles. Why is turning to God during times of trouble a good idea?

How was Moses similar to the lonesome stranger who helps out people in a Western?

How was he different?

How did Jesus fulfill the role of the lonesome stranger?

Session One: Ultimate Plan

How did Jesus totally break the mold?

How did what God did through Moses in the Exodus and what God did through Jesus in the New Testament help fulfill God's plan for us?

Note

1. "Memorable Quotes for *High Noon*," IMDb, 1990-2012. http://www.imdb.com/title/tt0044706/quotes (accessed June 28, 2012). The line is spoken by the judge in the town.

SESSION TWO

ULTIMATE POWER

Exodus 3–4

SESSION FOCUS

God used His power to help Moses. Jesus' power is big enough to help us—no matter what.

KEY VERSE

In this world you will have trouble. But take heart! I have overcome the world.

JOHN 16:33

SESSION AT A GLANCE

Section	60 Min.	90 Min.	What You Will Do
Getting started	10	15	Pray and worship
Main points of the chapter	25	35	Discuss the biblical dimensions of God's power as revealed to Moses and by Jesus
Application and discussion	15	25	Discuss personal application questions
Looking ahead	5	5	Prepare for next week
Wrapping up	5	10	Close with prayer or song

In human history, cultures have put a lot of stock in the power of arms. This has been especially true since the invention of gunpowder. Who's got the biggest, best, fastest guns usually settles matters. To a high degree, we depend on our military and police forces for our existence and survival—to defend us, to keep us safe and to keep the peace. We allow those forces to have the power to do good with it, so such power is not necessarily a bad thing, but it *is* a human thing.

Westerns, though, are different. The protagonists in Westerns are generally not dependent on military or police forces. They are individuals coping against odds that are stacked against them, depending on their wits and their skill with a gun. They are confident in their own power, and they are sure that it is by their own power that they will win or lose. Sometimes they take justice into their own hands and take their own revenge, which, given the context of the storyline, seems fair and good at the time. The individual's power is used for the greater good. But it *is* still human power.

HUMAN POWER

The Bible explains that human power is not the power on which we should depend: "Some trust in chariots and some in horses, but we trust in the name of the LORD our God" (Psalm 20:7). Even though David, the author of the psalm just quoted, was a warrior who used all his ingenuity, all the technology available during his time, and all the tricks of the trade to win his battles, he knew with whom the ultimate power lay: God.

The Bible repeatedly cautions against trusting in human power altogether, whether that power is displayed in a force of arms, the rulers who send the arms out, or anything made by human hands:

> It is better to take refuge in the LORD than to trust in man. It is better to take refuge in the LORD than to trust in princes (Psalm 118:8-9).

> Do not put your trust in princes, in mortal men, who cannot save (Psalm 146:3).

> [The LORD's] pleasure is not in the strength of the horse, nor his delight in the legs of a man; the Lord delights in those who fear him, who put their hope in his unfailing love (Psalm 147:10-11).

> Woe to those who go down to Egypt for help, who rely on horses, who trust in the multitude of their chariots and in the great strength of their horsemen, but do not look to the Holy One of Israel, or seek help from the LORD (Isaiah 31:1).

This seeming repudiation of human power does not mean that believers will never use the power they possess; they can and do use it in all sorts of ways, including to overcome evil. But the Bible teaches that *depending on human power* is to put our confidence in an idol, a false god; and the Bible is quite clear that we are to "have no other gods before" the Lord (Exodus 20:3).

GOD'S POWER

God, of course, uses His power in all sorts of ways, and it isn't always displayed in the use of force; force is not God's only strategy, and it's not God's "always" strategy. Sometimes God works quietly and behind the scenes. Sometimes God uses people who are imperfect by human standards. God reserves the right to use the weak things of the world to accomplish what He wants accomplished (see 1 Corinthians 1:26-31).

In one sense, the Bible's message can ultimately be boiled down to "God wins." But in the process, it often may look to us as if "God is losing." That's because of the inverted way God sometimes works in our world. Sometimes God's display of power creates a big splash and lots of glory. Sometimes His power is shown through weakness and humbleness.

There is no question that God is powerful. God created the heavens and the earth, so no one should ever doubt that God has immense capabilities (see Genesis 1:1). God is also good (see Mark 10:18). But God's goodness is something of a two-edged sword: If God is *for* good (see Genesis 50:20), then God must be *against* evil in all its forms. And that means that God is not always warm and fuzzy; God does use hardship or rebuke to get humans' attention.

The result is that our beliefs about God and good should not be measured by our experience of life, but that our experience of life should be measured by our faith in the ultimate goodness and justice of our all-powerful God.

And this means that things are not always as they seem.

RELUCTANT MOSES

Moses wasn't seeking to be a hero. He was just tending sheep and got curious when he saw a burning bush, so he decided to see what this strange thing was about. Then the voice of the Lord came out of the bush: Moses was to come no closer and was to remove his sandals because the place was holy ground. God then identified Himself, and Moses got scared, so he hid his face.

God then told Moses His motive for calling Moses. God had seen the misery of His people and felt compassion for them; He wanted to rescue them from the Egyptians and bring them into "a land flowing with milk and honey" (Exodus 3:8). Then God said to Moses, "So now, go. I am sending you to Pharaoh to bring my people the Israelites out of Egypt" (Exodus 3:10).

At this, Moses started making excuses. His first excuse was, "I'm a nobody. Who am I to do such an amazing thing?" God answered that He would be with Moses and God gave Moses a promise that the Israelites would worship on that very mountain, Mount Sinai. Then Moses asked a fair question: "Who should I say sent me?" God had identified Himself as the God of Abraham, Isaac and Jacob, but He had not revealed His personal name to Moses. God answered, "I AM WHO I AM. . . . Say to the Israelites: 'I AM has sent me to you'" (Exodus 3:14). Then God repeated His instruction to Moses and added that the Israelites would not leave Egypt empty-handed but with gold and other provisions from the Egyptians. This would be a second sign.

Moses thought about that and protested, "What if no one listens to me?" The Lord gave Moses three other signs of His (God's) power: (1) Moses'

OLD WEST CHARACTERS
WYATT EARP (1848–1929)

Wyatt Earp was an assistant city marshal in Dodge City, Kansas, before moving to Tombstone, Arizona, with his brothers, James and Virgil. Once there, the Earps clashed with a group of outlaws, culiminating in the famous "Gunfight at the O.K. Corral" on October 26, 1881. The 30-second gunfight—generally regarded as the most famous in the American Old West—was largely unknown to the public until author Stuart Lake published a largely fictionalized biography of Earp two years after his death. Today, Earp has the reputation of being "the toughest and deadliest gunman of his day."

Photo: Heritage Auction Gallery, date unknown. Public domain.

staff turned into a snake and then back into a staff; (2) Moses' hand turned leprous but was instantly restored; (3) water from the Nile turned into blood when poured on the ground (see Exodus 4:1-8).

Then Moses said, "But I'm not eloquent." At this point the Lord's answer was a bit short: "Who gave man his mouth? Who makes him deaf or mute? Who gives him sight or makes him blind? Is it not I, the LORD? Now go; I will help you speak and will teach you what to say" (Exodus 4:11-12). Moses' last desperate attempt to get out of his assignment was to say, "Please send someone else" (Exodus 4:13). God was *not* pleased with Moses' response, but He did give Moses his brother, Aaron, to be his spokesman.

Moses had no more excuses. Now he would have to return to Egypt. He first checked in with his father-in-law, Jethro; then, with his wife and family and Aaron, Moses went back to Egypt, gathered the elders of Israel, told them what God had said and showed them the signs from God. When they saw the signs and heard that God really cared about them and their misery, the elders believed, bowed down and worshiped God.

Like the hero in a Western, Moses certainly seemed to be just one individual trying to cope against odds that were stacked against him in the form of the pharaoh and the rest of the Egyptians. Unlike the hero in a Western, however, Moses was not at all confident in his own abilities, and he had been worried about how other people would react to him. Although he would be acting for the greater good—like a Western hero—he recognized that he was not up to the task. He didn't believe that he had the power and abilities to do what God wanted him to do. And that was part of God's point: Moses needed to look beyond his own resources; he had God and His power to help him.

THE NAME "I AM"

According to John 8:12-59, Jesus had a rather heated exchange with the Jewish religious leaders, concerning who Jesus said He was. Near the end of the conversation, the religious leaders claimed that they were the rightful children, or descendants, of Abraham and that they had God as their Father, whereas Jesus was not just an imposter but was also demon-possessed.

Jesus answered that on the contrary: "I honor my Father," the last two words being a phrase that indicated that Jesus had a special relationship with God the Father that the religious leaders did not have (John 8:49). Furthermore, Jesus said that He was not seeking His own glory, but God's, who is the judge of all. Then Jesus upped the ante, saying, "If anyone keeps my word, he will never see death" (John 8:51).

The religious leaders thought that this comment left little doubt that Jesus was demon-possessed. They said to Him that Abraham (the father of the Jewish people) had died, so they couldn't understand why Jesus could claim that He was greater than Abraham. Jesus replied that He didn't glorify Himself, but the Father did.

Then Jesus said something that, given the context, astounded His listeners: "Your father Abraham rejoiced at the thought of seeing my day; he saw it and was glad" (John 8:56). How could Jesus know this? The religious leaders knew that what Jesus was saying wasn't in the Bible, so they thought they had Him dead to rights:

> "You are not yet fifty years old," the Jews said to him, "and you have seen Abraham!" "I tell you the truth," Jesus answered, "before Abraham was born, I AM!" (John 8:57-58).

Jesus assigned to His own person the personal name of God that God had revealed to Moses on Mount Sinai (see Exodus 3:14)! The religious leaders then picked up stones to stone Jesus and thus carry out the required punishment for claiming to be God (see Leviticus 24:14). But Jesus escaped.

JESUS' POWER

Jesus said we need to have courage because He knows that in this world we will have troubles, face struggles, lose confidence, doubt our abilities, feel inadequate—times when we are not like the hero of the Western who is so sure of his own power to win the day. But we don't have to be the hero who has only his own wits and abilities on which to depend. We have available to us God and His power. The very same power that raised Jesus Christ from the dead, that is superior to this world, is ready to hold us up, to see us through, to give us the right words—to be the I AM when we are so assuredly the we-are-not. Jesus did not abandon us. Because of His victory over death, He is with us until we too have victory over death.

REFLECTION QUESTIONS

"Vengeance is mine; I will repay, saith the LORD" (Romans 12:19, *KJV*). How does this statement square with Westerns in general?

Why does it feel so good to see that the bad guys "get what's coming to them" at the end of a typical Western storyline?

What are some ways that people today deal with injustices?

Briefly describe a situation in which you felt that someone had wronged you. What did you do about the situation? What did you do to right the wrong that was done? How did you deal with the person who did the wrong?

Moses was a reluctant deliverer, even though God gave Moses ample displays of His power. How do you account for this?

Why is it okay to sometimes rely on your own power to successfully meet some challenge or solve a problem? How do God and His power fit into such a situation?

How can we apply the experience of the Israelites to our own lives today?

Why was Jesus correct when He claimed to be I AM, and what does that name mean to you?

Session Two: Ultimate Power

God worked through huge, obvious miracles to deliver His people from slavery in Egypt. God won. On the cross, Jesus submitted to humiliation, torture and death. It appeared that God had "lost." However, God is all-powerful, and He is the source of our power. How do you explain this apparent contradiction?

What hope do you derive from the resurrection power of Jesus operating in you?

SESSION THREE

ULTIMATE RESCUE

Exodus 5–12

SESSION FOCUS

God saved the Israelites from slavery in Egypt. Jesus' death and resurrection can save us from sin and give us eternal life.

KEY VERSE

I am the resurrection and the life. He who believes in me will live, even though he dies.

JOHN 11:25

SESSION AT A GLANCE

Section	60 Min.	90 Min.	What You Will Do
Getting started	10	15	Pray and worship
Main points of the chapter	25	35	Discuss the Exodus and how it parallels what Jesus does for us
Application and discussion	15	25	Discuss personal application questions
Looking ahead	5	5	Prepare for next week
Wrapping up	5	10	Close with prayer or song

Typical of most Westerns, either in literature or film, is the storyline of people suffering an injustice and in desperate need of rescuing. Order must be corrected, rights maintained and evil vanquished. Justice must prevail, and the lone stranger is just the person to accomplish the task.

RESCUE IN THE OLD WEST

At the turn of the previous century, Zane Grey made himself famous by writing novels and stories, mainly about the Old West. In *Rangers of the Lone Star*, the setting is Fairdale, a town named after a rich valley in a remote western part of frontier Texas. Although the town was characterized by its lawlessness, the leading citizens were reluctant to let the Texas Rangers "rescue" it and clean things up; they liked things just as they were. But even those townsfolk who did want things cleaned up were suspicious of the Texas Rangers. These lawmen had developed a reputation for operating above, beyond and against the law. As the governor in the novel puts it:

> As a whole they are a lot of swashbuckling adventurers and gunfighters, looking for somebody to kill. The sentiment in certain parts of the state makes heroes out of them, a fact which they are not slow to take advantage of. They have too much power. They are too much a law unto themselves. . . . There is a bill pending in the legislature now for the abolishment of this ranger service.[1]

One of the Rangers in the story is Captain MacNeal, a character modeled after real-life Texas Ranger Captain Leander H. McNelly, who got rid of the outlaw bands that infested Pecos County and restored the Texas Rangers to respectable status. In the story, MacNeal says that mere sheriffs or militias would not be up to the job of cleaning up the frontier. Sheriffs were men appointed to keep law already established; and militias were groups of men under military orders. Neither group could be as resourceful and, if necessary, crafty as Texas Rangers. Only Rangers were brave enough, steely enough and, if necessary, crafty enough to outwit and outshoot the outlaws and to establish lawful order:

> Sheriffs cannot deal with the situation as it stands today. There's a horde of criminals along the Rio Grande. I have a record of three thousand. The Panhandle and Staked Plains are also overrun by outlaws and desperadoes. There are honest communities . . . towns . . . whole counties under the dominance of clever, unscrupulous rustlers. A band of militia could not clean up these places. If it is to be done, the rangers must do it.[2]

Obviously, MacNeal's opinion will shortly be put to the test as he goes to Fairview in order to do his job and rescue the town.

Similarly, in the movie *The Western Code*, Tim Barrett is the man who does the rescuing, in this case of Polly Loomis, a damsel in distress. Nick Grindel is Polly's evil stepfather. He married Polly's mother shortly before the mother died but with sufficient time for the mother to have written a will leaving everything to him. Now Grindel wants to marry Polly, and Polly's brother wants Nick dead. Tim questions the legitimacy of the will, and eventually he investigates Nick's murder.

Both the town of Fairdale and the fair Polly are under the thrall of evil individuals, and both are in need of injustice to be rectified. The hero must "save the day."

RESCUE IN EXODUS

The book of Exodus is not a Western. But there are similarities with the stories we have just mentioned.

The themes of injustice and deliverance are obvious between the two. People who are afflicted and oppressed by violent men are freed. In the Westerns described above, the people who need deliverance are the townspeople and a damsel (and her brother) in distress. In the book of Exodus, the Israelites were suffering at the hands of Pharaoh and his Egyptian slave-masters.

Another similarity between the Westerns and the book of Exodus is the fact that unchecked corrupted power adversely affects relationships and damages individuals and society. Just as the head honchos in Fairdale were happy with the status quo, so too Pharaoh and the ruling classes benefitted from and didn't want to get rid of the free slave labor of the Israelites.

ENCOUNTERS WITH POWER

A third similarity between the Westerns and the book of Exodus is the encounter with power. In a Western, the climax of the story is very often a power encounter: a duel or a gunfight between the protagonist(s) and the antagonist(s). One's power, or ability, with a gun determines the outcome.

In Exodus, the Egyptians encountered the power of God, and the outcome was a forgone conclusion: God demonstrated His power over the false gods of Egypt. In other words, it was not just Pharaoh and powerful Egyptians who were oppressing the Israelites; Pharaoh and the Egyptians had given themselves over to the worship of false gods, who themselves put people under slavery and oppression. God not only wanted the Israelites to know Him (see Exodus 6:7; 10:2; 11:7), but He also wanted the Egyptians—including Pharaoh and his officials—to know that He is the true God (see Exodus 7:5; 8:10,22; 9:30).

In the book of Exodus, there are several power encounters between God and the Egyptians' gods and the magic practiced in Egypt. At their first meeting with Pharaoh, Moses and Aaron were unsuccessful in their attempt to convince Pharaoh to let God's people leave Egypt. In fact, things got worse for the Israelites, because they not only still had to make bricks, but also they now had to gather the straw needed to make the bricks—the same number of bricks as when straw had been supplied to them. This did not endear Moses and Aaron to the Israelites (see Exodus 5), but God still promised that He would prove His power by freeing the Israelites from Egyptian slavery, redeeming them and saving them (see Exodus 6:6-8). According to Exodus 7, Aaron used his rod to demonstrate superiority over the Egyptians' magic arts (see verses 1-13), and the Lord turned the Nile, considered by the Egyptians to be a god, into blood (see verses 14-24). This was the first of the 10 plagues.

The next plague was the plague of frogs, and through this plague God humiliated another of the Egyptian gods (see Exodus 7:25–8:14). However, after the frogs finally died, Pharaoh's heart hardened, and he would not let the people go (see Exodus 8:15). That same basic pattern was re-

OLD WEST CHARACTERS
MARY FIELDS (c. 1832–1914)

Mary Fields, also known as "Stagecoach Mary," was the first African-American woman employed as a mail carrier in the United States. Fields obtained the job in 1895 at the age of 60 because she was the fastest applicant to hitch a team of six horses. She drove her route from Cascade to St. Peter's Mission in Montana for several years and, despite heavy snowfalls that sometimes forced her to deliver mail on foot, never once missed a day. She retired at the age of 70 and ultimately became a respected public figure in the town of Cascade. She died in 1914, at just over the age of 80, from liver failure.

Photo: Unknown, circa 1895. Public domain.

peated with each of the other plagues: gnats, flies, livestock, boils, hail, locusts and darkness. The death of the firstborn—the last plague—was the turning point.

Knowing what was to come, Moses and Aaron repeated to the Israelites God's specific instructions about the last meal they were to have in Egypt and what they were to do with the blood of the slaughtered animals. During the night, God would come and take the firstborn of every Egyptian, but God would spare ("pass over"—Exodus 12:13) the homes that had lambs' blood spread on the tops of the doors and on the doorframes. The Israelites were to eat the Passover meal quickly in order to make good their escape.

In Egyptian thinking, Pharaoh himself was considered divine, so the death of the firstborn was a direct repudiation from God of Pharaoh's claims to divinity. And it was with this last plague that Pharaoh finally capitulated to God's demand to free His people.

DESTRUCTION VERSUS DELIVERANCE

A fourth similarity between Western stories and the book of Exodus is that in both storylines, two value systems are in direct conflict. In the Western stories, it's either lawlessness, or law and order; the violent will get everything they want or the violent will be prevented from getting everything they want; there will be either destruction or deliverance. Similarly, in the book of Exodus, it's either false gods or the one true God; pagan worship that will lead to death or worship of God who promises eternal life; destruction or deliverance. "There ain't room enough in this town" for both the false gods and the one true God.

The 10 plagues and miraculous escape from Egypt provide the basis for the first of the Ten Commandments: "I am the LORD your God, who brought you out of Egypt, out of the land of slavery. You shall have no other gods before me" (Exodus 20:2-3). This is one of the biggest lessons of the book of Exodus—and a lesson taught throughout the rest of the Old Testament.

RESCUE THROUGH JESUS

So how does this all relate to Jesus and the salvation that He made possible for us?

Not only is Jesus linked to God the Father as God the Son, but also Jesus is strongly identified with the people of Israel. According to Exodus 4:22, God called Israel "my firstborn son." But as the history of Israel progressed, the nation failed to live up to this high calling, falling multiple times into miserable disobedience and idolatry, rejecting the God who loves and redeems. On the other hand, in the New Testament, Jesus is called God's Son, the perfectly obedient One (see John 3:16; Hebrews 5:8).

The Gospel of Matthew records that when Jesus was an infant, Jesus' family moved to Egypt, which was where the Israelites were at the opening of the book of Exodus. Matthew quoted Hosea 11:1 and at the same time recalled the Exodus when he said that Jesus' family stayed in Egypt until after the death of Herod:

> An angel of the Lord appeared to Joseph in a dream. "Get up," he said, "take the child and his mother and escape to Egypt. Stay there until I tell you, for Herod is going to search for the child to kill him." So he got up, took the child and his mother during the night and left for Egypt, where he stayed until the death of Herod. And so was fulfilled what the Lord had said through the prophet: "Out of Egypt I called my son" (Matthew 2:13-15).

The New Testament also explicitly identifies Jesus' sacrifice on the cross with the Passover of Exodus 12: "For Christ, our Passover lamb, has been sacrificed. Therefore let us keep the Festival" (1 Corinthians 5:7-8). So we see that the New Testament links Jesus to the Exodus event, while at the same time expanding it and reinterpreting it. The Passover was prophetic in its own right; but with a new layer of New Testament meaning, "Egypt" becomes symbolic of sin, and the "Passover lamb" becomes symbolic of the sacrifice necessary to free us from our sins. Jesus rescued us from slavery to the devil just as God rescued the Israelites from slavery to the Egyptians. Jesus also rescued us from the destruction we would face because of our sins—actual death.

The Bible teaches that the result of sin is death (see Genesis 2:17; Proverbs 19:16; Ezekiel 18:20; 33:9; Romans 6:23). "Death" doesn't just mean physical death; it means separation from fellowship with God. By freeing us from our sins, Jesus also freed us from the curse of death. And as our memory verse, John 11:25, reminds us, Jesus is the One who will resurrect us to new life and will bring us into eternal life.

SESSION THREE: ULTIMATE RESCUE

REFLECTION QUESTIONS

At the beginning of many Westerns, people are often depicted as doing nothing to stop bad things from happening. Why do you think "good" people allow bad things to happen?

Why do you think the Israelites never rebelled against the Egyptians?

How is conflict in typical Western stories similar to the Exodus story? How is the conflict different?

Rescue from dire circumstances or deliverance from oppression comes from actions by humans and/or by God. In Westerns, from where does rescue or deliverance usually come?

In the book of Exodus, from where did rescue or deliverance come? What roles did Moses and Aaron play in the rescue of the Israelites?

What was God trying to get the Israelites and the Egyptians to realize, and why was this so important for both of them?

What does Jesus' own name mean (see Matthew 1:23), and since "Jesus" is the Greek form of "Joshua," what does "Joshua" mean? What does the meaning of Jesus' name tell us about God's agenda for Jesus and our partnership with Jesus in this life?

Briefly describe how Jesus is both like and different from the nation of Israel described in Exodus 5–12.

Session Three: Ultimate Rescue

Do you think death is an appropriate punishment for a sin? Why or why not?

How has Jesus changed your attitude and your lifestyle with regard to sin and death?

Notes
1. *Rangers of the Lone Star* (1914; Unity, Maine: Five Star Standard Print Western Series, 1997), p. 14.
2. Ibid., p. 15.

SESSION FOUR

ULTIMATE TRUST

Exodus 16–17:7

SESSION FOCUS

The Israelites could trust God to provide for them. We can trust Jesus to take care of us every day.

KEY VERSE

I am the bread of life. He who comes to me will never go hungry, and he who believes in me will never be thirsty.

JOHN 6:35

SESSION AT A GLANCE

Section	60 Min.	90 Min.	What You Will Do
Getting started	10	15	Pray and worship
Main points of the chapter	25	35	Discuss why we can trust that God will provide for us
Application and discussion	15	25	Discuss personal application questions
Looking ahead	5	5	Prepare for next week
Wrapping up	5	10	Close with prayer or song

Louis L'Amour, the great writer of Westerns, wrote the following lines about the desert:

> It is written in the memories of the ancient peoples that one who chooses the desert for his enemy has chosen a bitter foe, but he

who accepts it as friend, who will seek to understand its moods and whims, shall feel also its mercy, shall drink deep of its hidden waters, and the treasures of its rocks shall be opened before him. Where one may walk in freedom and find water in the arid places, another may gasp out his last breath under the desert sun and mark the sands with the bones of his ending.[1]

In Westerns, the desert—with its mountain ranges, basins, cliffs, ravines and sparse water—often becomes a character in the story. The human characters of the story are tested in the context of—and against—the desert's extremes. The key to surviving in the desert is knowing the ways of the desert. If you take the time to do this, you will understand the desert's moods, "feel . . . its mercy," "drink deep of its hidden waters," and find "the treasures of its rocks." One wonders if L'Amour wasn't borrowing biblical imagery in these words. But the Israelites had no time to become desert-wise as they started their exodus from Egypt. For them (as it is for us), the key was knowing God, for in coming to know and understand God, they would feel His mercy, drink deep from His waters and have His treasure of blessings open before them. The Israelites in the desert had to learn to trust only God.

TRUST IN THE EVOLUTION OF WESTERNS

If the desert is something of a constant in Westerns, the characters and storylines in Westerns, particularly films, have done a lot of evolving from their earliest days to the present.

TRADITIONAL WESTERNS

Traditional Westerns, which some say actually began with the dime novels of the 1860s, became an established genre by the turn of the twentieth century and have actually continued to the present day. Basically, they are usually simple morality tales, with good and bad clearly defined. Film examples include *The Great Train Robbery*, *Red River* and *High Noon*. The characters themselves may be complex, but the overall moral structure of how things should be—and the source of moral conflict—is assumed and is based, to a large extent, on Christian values. It is easy to tell who the good guys are (they usually wear white hats) and who the bad guys are (they usually wear black hats). One knows whom to trust.

However—and this is a big "however"—these traditional Westerns often contain misinterpretations about Indians, Mexicans and blacks as being inferior to the white "civilized" people—and are therefore inherently dangerous, cannot be trusted and must be subdued by their white "superiors." These kinds of assumptions are glaring in some traditional Westerns but muted in others. And some Western films held on to some assumptions while they also tried to explore the validity of others. John Ford's Academy Award-winning movie *Stagecoach* critiques social snobbery and hypocrisy at the same time that it tells the tale of a group of strangers riding on a stagecoach through dangerous Indian territory; in the movie *Fort Apache*, the Captain York character is torn between his duty as a military officer and his respect for the nearby Indians, with whom he has developed good relations, while at the same time the white trader is portrayed as a greedy destroyer who sells whiskey to and cheats the Indians.

Because traditional Westerns support traditional moral values and are in effect morality tales, they have an unfortunate tendency to ignore or downplay the real history of the Old West. There is little or no mention of such things as the Indian Removal Act of 1830 (think of the Trail of Tears); the broken treaties between the U.S. government and many of the Native American nations; the massacres of Native American men, women and children by either the U.S. Army or groups of white citizens (think of Sand Creek, Colorado, or Wounded Knee, South Dakota).

Revisionist Westerns

In the 1960s, new kinds of Westerns emerged, ones in which the morality is not so clear-cut. In these Westerns, the protagonists are not so noble or moral; in fact, they can be downright immoral and despicable. Their main motives are revenge, money or power—they are more antiheroic than heroic. Sergio Leone excelled at directing this sort of film, creating what became known as Spaghetti Westerns (think *A Fistful of Dollars* and *The Good, the Bad, and the Ugly*). And in such films as *Butch Cassidy and the Sundance Kid*, it was easy to forget that the handsome, loveable protagonists were actually lawless bank robbers.

From the 1970s to the present, the Western has continued to evolve. *Dances with Wolves* gave us a story in which a military officer eventually finds friends, love and a home among a tribe of Native Americans. *Blazing Saddles* parodied both the Western genre itself and racism. More recent offerings have included *Unforgiven*, a violent film about killing that questions the motives of the violence it depicts; *Tombstone*, a film about lawless lawmen; and *3:10 to Yuma*, a film about injustice, greed and honor on the part of both the guardians of society and an outlaw.

In a way, even though these revisionist Westerns may make us feel uncomfortable and cause us to wonder what the message is that each is trying to convey, they may be truer to the ambiguities, mixed motives and various roles played by the members of our society. One has to question whom to trust.

THE ISRAELITES' TRUST IN GOD

Whom to trust was a question the Israelites seemed to repeatedly ask themselves. When the Israelites made their escape from Egypt, the Egyptian army was hot on their heels, but God gave them victory over Pharaoh's chariots and horsemen, and the Israelites celebrated. At first glance, it might seem as if the Bible is giving us a traditional Western scenario, with Moses and the Israelites wearing the white hats and the Egyptians wearing the black hats. But it's not really quite that clear-cut.

TRAIL DUST
The Egyptians were not all bad. Joseph had been given an Egyptian wife (see Genesis 41:45) and had had considerable influence in Egypt. Also, the

OLD WEST CHARACTERS
DAVY CROCKETT (1786–1836)

David Crockett, the "King of the Wild Frontier," was a frontiersman, soldier and politician. At the age of 13 he ran away from home and spent the next three years roaming from town to town in Tennessee, where he learned many of his skills as a hunter and trapper. He joined the Tennessee Militia in 1813 and was elected to Congress in 1826. While in office he was a vocal critic of the policies of Andrew Jackson (most notably the Indian Removal Act), which led to his defeat in 1834. He moved to Texas (then an independent state of Mexico) and was killed at the Battle of the Alamo in March 1836.

Photo: Painting by John Gadsby Chapman (1808-1889). Public domain.

Egyptians had made a hospitable place for the Hebrews in Goshen, a very nice piece of land (see Genesis 47:6). And, "many other people" (a "mixed multitude" according to *KJV*) actually joined the Hebrews on their journey out of Egypt (Exodus 12:38).

On the other hand, the Israelites were not all good. At the first sign of trouble, not long after crossing the Red Sea on dry land, the Israelites began to grumble, essentially questioning whether Moses (and by extension God) was worthy of their trust (see Exodus 15:24). The white hats the Israelites "wore" quickly became covered with the dust of distrust.

Provision

In most Westerns, the characters always seem to have plenty of provisions or at least seem to easily procure something to eat. When the Israelites were on the threshold of the desert, they didn't have much in the way of food. They had unleavened bread and whatever meat they would procure from the flocks and herds they had brought along (see Exodus 12:38). But they were in the desert, and the desert didn't have much water—and neither did the people. So, as previously mentioned, the people grumbled. The Lord made the water at Marah drinkable and then led them to the oasis of Elim, where there was plenty of water and shade (see Exodus 15:27).

Sometime between the rest at Elim and the next stage of their journey, though, the Israelites had apparently used up all the food that they could get from their flocks and herds, because Exodus 16 opens with the people again grumbling, this time against both Moses and Aaron: "If only we had died by the LORD's hand in Egypt! There we sat around pots of meat and ate all the food we wanted, but you have brought us out into this desert to starve this entire assembly to death" (Exodus 16:3). Instead of trusting in God, the people looked for the easiest way out of their predicament.

Moses prayed to God, and God provided flocks of quail for the people to eat in the evening and manna for the people to collect and eat in the morning (see Exodus 16:13-15). God instructed each person to take only what he or she needed for the day; but on the day before the Sabbath, they could take enough for two days. If they tried to collect more, it would go bad.

The provision was miraculous, but there is an edge to the story: The Lord was angry with the people because they had grumbled against Moses, for grumbling against Moses amounted to grumbling against God Himself (see Exodus 16:8). Despite this, as a sign of God's mercy, the Lord's glory appeared in the cloud that guided the Israelites by day (see Exodus 16:10). The people, however, still did not really trust in God.

According to Exodus 17, even though God showed His daily mercy and faithfulness to the people with His miraculous provisions, when the people were in Rephidim, they again grumbled about the lack of drinkable water. They demanded that Moses give them water and hotly accused Moses of bringing them to the desert only to die. Moses recognized what was going on—and so did God. This complaining amounted to accusing God Himself that He cared nothing for them. The Lord told Moses to go to the rock at Horeb and strike it with his staff, and water would come from the rock. The place was named Massah and Meribah (meaning "testing" and "rebellion," respectively).

OUR TRUST IN JESUS

During the Exodus, God provided food for His people in the harsh desert. In the New Testament, Jesus provided food for us: He is "the bread of life" (John 6:35,48) and "living water" (John 4:10; 7:38). Later, Paul wrote that in the wilderness the Israelites "ate the same spiritual food and drank the same spiritual drink; for they drank of the spiritual rock that accompanied them" (1 Corinthians 10:3-4). Who was this spiritual rock? "That rock was Christ" (1 Corinthians 10:4).

We must trust the Rock just as the Israelites did (most of the time). We are to "trust in the LORD forever, for the LORD, the LORD, is the Rock eternal" (Isaiah 26:4). Not only is Jesus eternal, but He also wants us to share eternity with Him:

> Very truly I tell you, the one who believes has eternal life. I am the bread of life. Your forefathers ate the manna in the desert, yet they died. But here is the bread that comes down from heaven, which a man may eat and not die. I am the living bread that came down from heaven. If anyone eats of this bread, he will live forever. This bread is my flesh, which I will give for the life of the world (John 6:47-51).

We simply need to believe in Jesus and trust Him each and every day—literally with our lives.

REFLECTION QUESTIONS

In what ways did the Egyptians typify Western characters who wore white hats? In what ways did they typify Western characters who wore black hats?

In what ways did the Israelites typify Western characters who wore white hats? In what ways did they typify Western characters who wore black hats?

How might the fact that we are all sinners influence our thinking about who is good and who is evil, or about injustice?

How do traditional Westerns simplify things in regard to justice and knowing whom to trust?

How do revisionist Westerns reflect our culture and society?

Why do you think the Israelites did not always trust God, even though they had seen Him perform miracles?

What are some of the things that people trust in this world? Why are these not necessarily dependable?

Why is God trustworthy?

Briefly compare a time when you trusted your own abilities and a time when you trusted God.

What's the difference between the food that God provided for the Israelites and the food provided by Jesus?

Note

1. Louis L'Amour, *The Collected Short Stories of Louis L'Amour: The Frontier Stories,* vol. 1 (New York: Bantam Dell, 2003), p. 76.

SESSION FIVE

ULTIMATE LOVE

Exodus 19–20:21; 24:12; 25:10-22

SESSION FOCUS

God gave commands for the Israelites to follow. Jesus' new command is to follow Him and love others.

KEY VERSES

A new command I give you: Love one another. As I have loved you, so you must love one another. By this all men will know that you are my disciples, if you love one another.

JOHN 13:34-35

SESSION AT A GLANCE

Section	60 Min.	90 Min.	What You Will Do
Getting started	10	15	Pray and worship
Main points of the chapter	25	35	Discuss what the Ten Commandments have to do with loving God and loving our fellow human beings
Application and discussion	15	25	Discuss personal application questions
Looking ahead	5	5	Prepare for next week
Wrapping up	5	10	Close with prayer or song

It's hard to separate Westerns from mountains. Whether you're on the flat of a desert or on the wide-open plains, the mountains are looming, or beckoning, there in the distance. They are a constant reminder of things that are large and immovable, of things that can't be changed but must be adjusted to. Climb high enough on a mountain and you'll lose your breath. Stay long enough on a mountain and you'll get very cold. It's the way of mountains to be irresistibly beautiful, uncompromisingly hard and not just a little threatening.

MOUNTAINS IN THE WESTERN

In his book *West of Dodge*, author Louis L'Amour gives us this picture of what mountains are like:

> Ahead of them, a deep gash broke the face of the plain, and without hesitation he rode into it. A thin stream trickled along the bottom, but that was merely the result of local rain. What was coming was back up there in those rock-sided mountains, where nothing stopped the weight of rushing water.[1]

In Westerns, the mountains are where wild animals and fierce tribes of Native Americans roam. Mountains provide hideouts for robbers and outlaws trying to escape the long arm of the law. Mountains may contain silver and/or gold, lusted after by both the honest and the unscrupulous. Mountains are the haunts of legendary mountaineers, or mountain men, loners unafraid of much of anything. When a Western character reaches the mountains, almost anything can happen, and one never knows exactly what the mountain has in store.

Mountains are where Western characters have powerful and often life-altering experiences.

THE MOUNTAIN OF THE LORD

Mountains are also where the Israelites had powerful, life-altering experiences—unforgettable, explosive, nerve-racking experiences with God, culminating with God's revelation to Moses of the Ten Commandments.

Preparation

In Exodus 19, at the foot of Mount Sinai, the Lord expressed His desire to Moses that the Israelites become His people, a holy nation dedicated to

Him alone. Moses relayed this message to the people, and with one voice they agreed, binding themselves to God (see Exodus 19:1-8).

God then told Moses to get the people ready for a serious dedication ceremony. They were to wash their clothes, keep to the boundaries that Moses was to set up near the mountain, abstain from sexual relations, and wait three days (see Exodus 19:9-15). As day broke on the third day, thunder, lightning, a thick cloud and a piercing trumpet blast assaulted the senses of the people. Then came smoke, fire and violent tremors on the mountain—and the trumpet blast grew louder:

> On the morning of the third day there was thunder and lightning, with a thick cloud over the mountain, and a very loud trumpet blast. Everyone in the camp trembled. Then Moses led the people out of the camp to meet with God, and they stood at the foot of the mountain. Mount Sinai was covered with smoke, because the LORD descended on it in fire. The smoke billowed up from it like smoke from a furnace, and the whole mountain trembled violently. As the sound of the trumpet grew louder and louder, Moses spoke and the voice of God answered him (Exodus 19:16-19).

The people were shaking with fright, and Moses was so frightened that he trembled with fear (see Hebrews 12:18-21).

Then the Lord again told Moses to warn the people that they risked death if they even touched the mountain. Even the priests were not allowed to come close. The only person Moses could bring with him to the mountaintop would be Aaron, his brother (see Exodus 19:20-24).

REVELATION

After the Israelites had followed all of God's instructions, the Lord finally got down to business. He laid down the law for Moses, literally: God told to Moses the Ten Commandments, the same commandments that would later be inscribed on stone (see Exodus 24:12; 31:18) and placed in the Ark of the Covenant (see Exodus 25:10-22).

The Ten Commandments are a revelation from God (see Exodus 20:1-17). They are a reminder from God of our higher calling as potential children of God. They are a reminder to us of the things that we already have known in our heart of hearts yet we may deny because of the deceptiveness of sin.

The important thing to realize is that in the first four commandments, God is looking for our wholehearted love of Him; in the last six, God is looking for our wholehearted love of our neighbors.

In retrospect, the pivotal importance for Western culture of this moment in history cannot be overestimated. On the social plane, the Ten Commandments provide the legal foundation for our concepts of human dignity, individual worth, and justice. On the spiritual plane, the importance is just as great, if not greater: We are told how to become holy.

THE ORIGINS OF ETHICS AND MORALS

For a moment, let us consider what human morals would look like if there had been no giving of the Ten Commandments.

If we consider the many different systems of laws that various cultures have today, we might be tempted to think that ethics and morals are arbitrary and purely relative. Maybe they are simply social constructs put in place and enforced by the powerful (the "winners," the mighty) to keep themselves in power and everyone else in his or her place. Maybe ethics and morals come into play only so that we get along with others better, possibly for an ulterior motive, like to make money in business. We might even be tempted to think that morals and ethics don't matter, or shouldn't matter, and that we should be able to do whatever we want, either without

OLD WEST CHARACTERS
BUFFALO BILL (1846–1917)

William Frederick Cody spent his early life as a frontiersman and hunter, but he is most renown for his work as a showman. Born in Iowa, he served in the U.S. Army from 1868 to 1872, where he was often employed as a scout or a hunter. He was awarded a Medal of Honor in 1872, and that year he made his stage debut in one of the original Wild West Shows. Ten years later he founded his own show, "Buffalo Bill's Wild West," which would influence many twentieth-century portrayls of the "Old West" in movies and books. He died in 1917 and was buried atop Lookout Mountain in Golden, Colorado.

Photo: Library of Congress (1911). Public domain.

any restrictions or with the only restriction being that what we do doesn't hurt anybody.

Along these lines, some Christians have argued that without God laying down the law, people would be amoral beasts, with no idea of right and wrong, utterly unrestrained in their behavior. Further, these Christians claim that atheists who try to hold to any sort of moral system are hypocrites because, for them, there can be no right or wrong; and survival of the fittest, or doing only what gives them an advantage or what is in their interests, should be the only values.

This kind of thinking among Christians is wrong because it does not account for two huge facts. First, there is the fact that God has created humans—men and women—in His image (see Genesis 1:26-27); therefore, corrupted and polluted though we may be by sin, we still have God's image—a glimpse of glory, reconciliation with God, justice, fairness, rightness and a desire for good—implanted in our souls.

Second, there is the fact that God has given each of us a conscience, itself susceptible to being corrupted by sin, but nevertheless an indicator in our souls that we know when we do wrong (see Romans 2:14-16).

When we Christians attempt to stake out the holier-than-thou high ground, the fact that others know our weaknesses all too well just makes us hypocrites.

All people know right from wrong, and to whatever extent they act on that difference, they will be judged by God. We are all to live up to God's standard, His image, that is in us.

LOVING OTHERS THE WAY THAT JESUS LOVES US

The fact we have God's image in us makes us unique in this world. We are different from every other thing and creature. But how can we sinners have been made in the image of God who is without sin? We have to remember that when God originally created people in His image, they too were without sin. Adam and Eve had yet to meet the serpent.

Fortunately, God gave us a way to again become without sin:

> All this is from God, who reconciled us to himself through Christ and gave us the ministry of reconciliation: that God was reconciling the world to himself in Christ, not counting men's sins

against them. And he has committed to us the message of reconciliation. . . . God made [Jesus] who had no sin to be sin for us, so that in him we might become the righteousness of God (2 Corinthians 5:18-19,21).

When we confess our sins and repent, God will forgive our sins. Then we must turn away from doing wrong and again follow God's commandments. As we try to follow God's commandments, we are in effect trying again to be like Jesus: holy and spotless. We are attempting to meet the standard of behavior set by Jesus. And one of Jesus' standards was the way He showed love.

Jesus' "new command" to "love one another" is not really new (John 13:34-35). It's actually a repetition of a command that God had given to the Israelites in Leviticus 19:15-18:

> Do not pervert justice; do not show partiality to the poor or favoritism to the great, but judge your neighbor fairly. Do not go about spreading slander among your people. Do not do anything that endangers your neighbor's life. I am the LORD. Do not hate a fellow Israelite in your heart. Rebuke your neighbor frankly so you will not share in their guilt. Do not seek revenge or bear a grudge against anyone among your people, but love your neighbor as yourself. I am the LORD.

But to love our neighbors as much as Jesus loves us was most certainly new. Jesus loves us so much that He willingly died for us. As the apostle Paul wrote in Romans 5:6-8:

> You see, at just the right time, when we were still powerless, Christ died for the ungodly. Very rarely will anyone die for a righteous person, though for a good person someone might possibly dare to die. But God demonstrates his own love for us in this: While we were still sinners, Christ died for us.

It is that attitude we are to live out. By following this one "new" command, we actually follow the last six Ten Commandments; and at the same time we show the world why we believe what we do. We live out our lives, showing the world the image of God that is in us.

SESSION FIVE: ULTIMATE LOVE

REFLECTION QUESTIONS

What is the significance of the mountains in the West? Why do you think it was appropriate that God spoke to His people while He was on a mountain?

What is the significance of the thunder, lightning and trumpet blast?

What is the significance of having the Israeliets prepare as they did?

In what ways do we prepare to meet God or hear Him speak?

Why was it appropriate that the people not be allowed to even touch the mountain when God was there?

How would you have felt if you had been at Mount Sinai when God spoke to Moses?

What are the first four commandments? How do they relate to loving God?

1.
2.
3.
4.

What are the last six commandments? How do these commandments relate to loving your neighbors?

5.
6.

Session Five: Ultimate Love

7.
8.
9.
10.

Why do you think that pride is sometimes considered the reason every commandment is broken?

Why is it so important that we show the world that we love others?

How do you feel about knowing you were made in God's image? What responsibility in you does that engender?

The Ten Commandments are, in general, things we are *not to do*. According to our memory verse, John 13:34-35, Jesus gave us one thing *to do*. What are a few practical things that you can do for a fellow human being to demonstrate your desire to express your love for him or her?

Note
1. Louis L'Amour, *West of Dodge* (New York: Bantam Books, 1996), p. 63.

SESSION SIX

ULTIMATE COURAGE

Genesis 37; 39

SESSION FOCUS

God was with Joseph and saw him through every trouble that he faced. Jesus is with us to guide us through every challenge that we face.

KEY VERSES

God is our refuge and strength, an ever-present help in trouble. Therefore we will not fear, though the earth give way and the mountains fall into the heart of the sea.

PSALM 46:1-2

SESSION AT A GLANCE

Section	60 Min.	90 Min.	What You Will Do
Getting started	10	15	Pray and worship
Main points of the chapter	25	35	Discuss how trials reveal character
Application and discussion	15	25	Discuss personal application questions
Looking ahead	5	5	Prepare for next week
Wrapping up	5	10	Close with prayer or song

A hallmark of most good stories is the exploration of the various characters and what motivates them to act as they do. From the situations in which people are put, we see what they're made of. Westerns are no exception in this regard, and neither is the Bible.

CHARACTER STUDIES IN WESTERNS

The William Munny character in the film *Unforgiven* seems to have been reformed from his once-violent ways by his good wife, but she dies. To gain some bounty money, he is reluctantly pulled into a cycle of violence again. Or take the Dan Evans character in *3:10 to Yuma*. With his young wife, he struggles to maintain his small farm and raise his children in the right way. After he witnesses a robbery, he helps escort the lead robber to the train. He does this in part for the reward money and in part to determine whether he is made of tougher-than-just-a-rancher fiber. He must eventually choose between showing immense courage and following through on what he said he'd do, or saving his skin but going back on his word.

It's not just the men who get the spotlight in these character studies. In the movie *High Noon,* the Amy Fowler character has just married the Marshall Will Kane character. They are about to go on their honeymoon when Kane hears that an outlaw whom he put away many years ago has gotten out of jail and is out for revenge. Amy leaves, challenging Will to choose between her and his honor. At this point, the Helen Ramirez character berates Amy for her attitude: "What kind of a woman are you? How could you leave him like this? Does the sound of guns frighten you that much?"[1]

Later, Helen and Amy have another conversation:

Helen: I don't understand you. No matter what you say. If Kane was my man, I'd never leave him like this. I'd get a gun. I'd fight.

Amy: Why don't you?

Helen: He is not my man. He's yours.[2]

And in the film *True Grit,* the character Mattie Ross, a young girl, sees her father gunned down by an outlaw. She then sets out to capture the outlaw with the help of a U.S. Marshall whom she hires. Mattie must determine whether she has the grit, or the courage, to see her plan through to the end.

Westerns continually ask, What are these characters made of? And through the magic of fictional drama, each member of the audience or each reader in turn must ask him- or herself: *What kind of a person am I? What would I have done in similar circumstances? What am I made of?*

MULTIPLE FACETS IN CHARACTERS

The more interesting and compelling Western characters are multifaceted, complicating the answer to the relatively simple question concerning what makes a character tick.

It is clear that William Munny's wife was a good and faith-filled woman. The love of this good woman had a good effect on the man—which often happens in Westerns—but William Munny had a very hard time completely escaping his past. The outlaw Ben Wade in *3:10 to Yuma* wasn't all bad: He could quote chapter and verse from the Bible, and he also developed a soft spot in his heart for the courageous but out-of-his-depth young rancher who was taking him in to face the law.

Amy Fowler answered Helen's question about the kind of woman she was with this retort:

> I've heard guns. My father and my brother were killed by guns. They were on the right side but that didn't help them any when the shooting started. My brother was nineteen. I watched him die. That's when I became a Quaker. I don't care who's right or who's wrong. There's got to be some better way for people to live. Will knows how I feel about it.[3]

Obviously, Amy's past experiences colored how she reacted to her current circumstances, so she prepared to leave town and her new husband. But when she heard gunfire, she returned to town and ultimately found the courage to help her husband save his life.

CHARACTER STUDIES IN THE BIBLE

The Bible is full of good stories about individual people, and even when the stories are short or the words are few, we can still learn a great deal about the character whose story or words we read. The book of Genesis is full of such character studies. Adam and Eve were born with silver spoons in their mouths. They had everything going for them, but they threw it all away. Nimrod was a mighty hunter, but he may have been the leader who encouraged the building of the Tower of Babel. Noah saved humanity, but the effects of wine made him behave immodestly. Abraham was a man of faith, but he was flawed by a streak of callousness and deception. Isaac followed in his father Abraham's footsteps—both good and bad. If Jacob were alive today, his name would be Black Bart, and you wouldn't want to buy a used car from him.

But one character study stands out from the rest: Joseph, the spoiled favorite son of Jacob. Although Jacob should have loved all his sons equally, he showered special affection only on Joseph. Jacob made his higher regard for Joseph especially obvious when he gave Joseph an ornate robe, whereas the other brothers had to get by with ordinary clothes. This favoritism got under the skin of the older brothers, and we can only imagine how their rage seethed against him. Unfortunately, Joseph, for his part, did nothing to alleviate their hatred.

Joseph's Dreams

At 17, Joseph was not without fault. In fact, Joseph, seemingly unaware of his own family's dysfunctional dynamics, foolishly aggravated things even more by sharing with his brothers two dreams he had had; in each of the dreams, the brothers ended up bowing down to him, a sign of obeisance reserved for a king or very high official. Needless to say, the brothers were not thrilled to hear the dreams that Joseph so happily described to them.

Dreams can be wild and wooly. But there is no doubt in the Bible that God can and does speak to people through dreams. In this case, the dreams about the sheaves and stars were from the Lord. They served as a foreshadowing of what would happen in the future. God had gifted Joseph with

Old West Characters
Annie Oakley (1860–1926)

"Annie Oakley," the stage name for Phoebe Ann Moses, was a sharpshooter and exhibition shooter. Born in a cabin in Ohio, she began shooting at the age of 8 to support her family. By 1885 her reputation in the region had grown to the point where she was asked to join Buffalo Bill's Wild West Show, where she performed tricks such as splitting a playing card in half and shooting more holes into it before it hit the ground. In 1902 she quit the show and took up acting, though she continued to set records into her sixties. After an auto accident in 1922 her health steadily declined, and she died in 1926.

Photo: Unknown (c. 1880s). Public domain.

the ability to interpret the future through the dreams; and at key points in the story, Joseph interpreted the dreams of various people—from commoners all the way up to Pharaoh, the king of Egypt.

Joseph's sharing of his dreams with his brothers set in motion a series of situations that would land Joseph in various depths of trouble—in at least one case, a literal depth. One day when Jacob sent Joseph to check on his brothers to see how the sheepherding was going, they plotted to kill him. Only the intervention of Reuben prevented them from making a fatal mistake. Instead of murdering Joseph, the brothers threw Joseph into a pit (literally a depth). Meanwhile, a caravan of Ishmaelite traders came by, and the brothers decided to sell Joseph to them. Then, when the traders got to Egypt, they sold Joseph to Potiphar, the captain of Pharaoh's palace guard. Meanwhile, the brothers soaked Joseph's ornate robe in sheep's blood and brought it back to Jacob, lying to him that Joseph had been killed by a wild animal. The brothers figured that they would never again have to deal with their pesky younger brother or his stupid dreams.

JOSEPH'S CHARACTER TESTS

We can only imagine the abuse, humiliation and hardship that Joseph underwent as a slave. But along with those troubles, which were bad enough, he also had to adapt to a new culture, learn a new language and become familiar with a way of life that was entirely new for him—all at a relatively young age. So the first test for Joseph was to see whether he could survive the ordeal of being enslaved.

The second test for Joseph was to see whether he could make the best of his bad situation. Joseph pitched in and used his God-given talents to serve Potiphar. As the Bible puts it: "The LORD was with Joseph and he prospered, and he lived in the house of his Egyptian master" (Genesis 39:2). Potiphar soon recognized that clearly here was a young man with considerable abilities: "When his master saw that the LORD was with him and that the LORD gave him success in everything he did, Joseph found favor in his eyes" (Genesis 39:3-4). Potiphar put Joseph in charge of the running of his whole house and of everything else he owned; and God blessed Potiphar "because of Joseph" (Genesis 39:5). Potiphar could trust Joseph because Joseph had integrity. In fact, Joseph was doing such a good job that Potiphar had to worry only about what he would eat (see Genesis 39:6). At this point, things seemed to be going relatively well and Joseph was making something pretty good out of his bad situation.

The third test for Joseph was trickier: It was to see whether his integrity and his obedience to God held true. Joseph was a handsome, well-built lad, and Potiphar's wife took a shine to him. Joseph must have known that he was in a no-win situation: If he gave in to the wife, she would have control over his fate. If he refused her, she could falsely accuse him of seducing her. Either way, his position at Potiphar's house was precarious. When the wife pressed Joseph and tried to seduce Joseph, he refused her advances, telling her, "How . . . could I do such a wicked thing and sin against God?" (Genesis 39:9).

Potiphar's wife continued to press her advances on the unwilling Joseph until one day she grabbed his cloak, and he ran away from her—leaving his cloak still in her hand. Probably very hurt and extremely angry and humiliated by his refusal to succumb to her advances, Potiphar's wife falsely accused Joseph of doing exactly what she had wanted and he had refused to do. Enraged, Potiphar had Joseph thrown into prison. As unjust as being thrown into prison was, Joseph *had* maintained his integrity and obedience to God.

The fourth test for Joseph had to do with weathering his new imprisonment. Joseph could easily have lapsed into despair, wondering, since he had done nothing wrong, why had his brothers hated him, why had he been sold into slavery, why had he been falsely accused of a crime, why had he been unjustly imprisoned. But Joseph didn't question his situation. Rather, he resolved to keep doing what he had been doing all along, just in the new setting. Before Joseph had been in prison very long, the warden put Joseph in charge of the prison. Just as Potiphar had had no worries with Joseph in charge, so too it was with the warden.

And the reason why Joseph was always able to have courage and accept every trouble that had befallen him? "The LORD was with Joseph and gave him success in whatever he did" (Genesis 39:23).

THE CHARACTER OF JESUS

The fact that God was with Joseph so that he was able to make the best of every trouble he faced should be an encouragement for us, because the Bible makes clear that God is always with us as well. Jesus said:

> If you love me, you will obey what I command. And I will ask the Father, and he will give you another Counselor to be with you for-

ever—the Spirit of truth. The world cannot accept him, because it neither sees him nor knows him. But you know him, for he lives with you and will be in you. I will not leave you as orphans; I will come to you. Before long, the world will not see me anymore, but you will see me. Because I live, you also will live. On that day you will realize that I am in my Father, and you are in me, and I am in you. Whoever has my commands and obeys them, he is the one who loves me. He who loves me will be loved by my Father, and I too will love him and show myself to him (John 14:15-21).

Jesus said these words not too long before He was crucified and died. Even though He was going to leave this earth, He said that He would be with us, because if we have the Holy Spirit in us (which we do as believers), then we also have Jesus in us. If we have Jesus in us, we have the same courage in us that He had when He died for us. We can have the courage to face every challenge that comes our way because we have Jesus to guide us. We simply have to turn to Him when we are in need.

REFLECTION QUESTIONS

Why are multifaceted characters more interesting to read about or watch in a film?

In what ways is Joseph a multifaceted character?

Do you think that the reaction of Joseph's brothers to Joseph's dreams was justified? Why or why not?

What do you believe about God speaking to people in dreams today? Give a reason for your answer.

Joseph went from being a favorite son to being sold as a slave and then falsely accused of a crime and thrown into prison. Do you think his story is far-fetched? Why or why not?

Briefly describe a time when you felt as if your character was being tested. What did you do in or about your challenging situation?

Session Six: Ultimate Courage

How did Joseph show courage, and what was the true source of his courage?

How did Jesus show courage?

Reread John 14:15-21. How can Jesus make us people of courage?

According to our memory verse, Psalm 46:1-2, when things get really challenging in our lives, what should we do, and why?

Notes
1. "Memorable Quotes for *High Noon*," *IMDb,* 1990-2012. http://www.imdb.com/title/tt0044706/quotes (accessed July 2012).
2. Ibid.
3. Ibid.

SESSION SEVEN

ULTIMATE MORAL COMPASS

Genesis 40–41

SESSION FOCUS

Joseph followed God's moral compass, and God delivered him from prison to a palace. Jesus is the model for our moral compass, and He delivers us from sin to eternal life.

KEY VERSE

No temptation has seized you except what is common to man. And God is faithful; he will not let you be tempted beyond what you can bear. But when you are tempted, he will also provide a way out so that you can stand up under it.

1 CORINTHIANS 10:13

SESSION AT A GLANCE

Section	60 Min.	90 Min.	What You Will Do
Getting started	10	15	Pray and worship
Main points of the chapter	25	35	Discuss codes of honor and their relationship to correct conduct
Application and discussion	15	25	
Looking ahead	5	5	Discuss personal application questions
Wrapping up	5	10	Prepare for next week
			Close with prayer or song

John Wayne once said, "A man's got to have a code, a creed to live by, no matter what his job."[1] This goes for both men and women. In general, a code of honor is a set of rules or principles that describe how a person should conduct him- or herself. The code of honor in operation is different for each community in which it is supposed to operate; but in any one community of people, a code of honor relies on all of those people acting honorably by following the rules. A president is supposed to defend the Constitution; a physician, to abide by the Hippocratic Oath; a police officer, to keep the peace using only necessary force; a scholar, to push the frontiers of knowledge. There is honor even among thieves.

THE WESTERN CODE OF HONOR

Cowboys also have a code of honor, a way to conduct themselves in order to assure survival:

> Back in the days when the cowman with his herds made a new frontier, there was no law on the range. Lack of written law made it necessary for him to frame some of his own, thus developing a rule of behavior which became known as the "Code of the West." These homespun laws, being merely a gentleman's agreement to certain rules of conduct for survival, were never written into statutes, but were respected everywhere on the range.[2]

The cowboys' code was not trivial or frivolous. And it had to do not just with manners but also with means of work and survival:

- Take care of your horse before you take care of yourself.
- A horse thief pays with his life for stealing a horse.
- Don't mount another man's horse, and never try on his hat.
- A cowboy never asks another cowboy about his past.
- Never pass anyone on the trail without saying "Howdy."[3]

Here are a few more of the "homespun laws":

- Remove your guns before sitting at the dining table.
- Never drink anything weaker than whiskey.
- Don't inquire into a person's past. Take the measure of a man for what he is today.
- Don't wave at a man on a horse, as it might spook the horse. A nod is the proper greeting.
- Cuss all you want, but only around men, horses, and cows.

- Never shoot an unarmed or unwarned enemy.
- Never shoot a woman no matter what.[4]

Cowboys, once known as cowpunchers (for the practice of branding cows) and drovers, were also known as "the men that knew cow."[5] And a cowboy didn't just "know cow"; he went "to the school of nature."[6] A cowboy's language was spiced with sayings that recognized the changeability and fickleness of nature, such as "God willing and the creek don't rise."[7] Speaking about a cowboy's life in nature and relating to the Code of the West, Theodore Roosevelt wrote:

> Sinewy, hardy, self-reliant, their life forces them to be both daring and adventurous, and the passing over their heads of a few years leaves printed on their faces certain lines which tell of dangers quietly fronted and hardships uncomplainingly endured.[8]

And Clint Eastwood once wrote: "Working cowboys are the embodiment of the true American spirit."[9] If we're Americans, we each contain some cowboy.

THE WEAKNESS OF ANY CODE OF HONOR

Similar to the Code of the West is a person's personal code of honor, which is his or her interior moral compass. Like the cowboys' code, it is informed by many things: culture, history, family, friends, peers and even nature. As such, it is a human product, as is the Code of the West. And being human products, they are subject to both the strengths and weaknesses of human nature.

A code of honor guides our conscience. Conscience is also a God-given gift. But our consciences, as well as our codes of honor, can be corrupted by the exceeding deceptiveness of sin. As Paul writes, "In order that sin might be recognized as sin, it used what is good to bring about my death, so that through the commandment sin might become utterly sinful" (Romans 7:13).

Therefore, even though our codes of honor and consciences have much good in them, we need to subject them to the scrutiny of God's Word and God's Spirit. God's Word helps us discern our duplicitous thoughts and motives (see Proverbs 21:2), and it reveals to us where we're not measuring up to God's Word (see John 16:8-11).

JOSEPH'S CODE OF HONOR

It is obvious that Joseph had a well-developed code of honor, or moral compass, because his life was a life well lived. The Bible doesn't tell us all that much about Joseph's interior life, but we do have a string of clues as to what was driving his own personal code of honor.

The first indication of Joseph's code of honor is found in Genesis 37:2: "Joseph ... brought their father a bad report about [his brothers]." We don't know what Joseph's brothers had done, but something they had done violated Joseph's sense of right and wrong. The second indication of Joseph's code is that early on, Joseph had some spiritual awareness that God might be speaking to him in dreams. He may have been unwise in sharing those dreams with his brothers and father, but at least he was paying attention.

The third indication of Joseph's code is that, like cowboys on the range, Joseph and his brothers took care of sheep out in the countryside. Most likely, Joseph would have been a student of nature, so he would have developed an attitude of awe toward the magnificence and wonder of all of nature. And since he was a person of faith, he probably realized that God deserved the credit and praise for the glory of His creation. The fourth

OLD WEST CHARACTERS

RED CLOUD (1822–1909)

Maȟpíya Lúta was chief of the Oglala Lakota (Sioux) from 1868 to 1909. He led a series of successful campaigns against the U.S. Army from 1866 to 1868, prompting troops to refer to the conflict as "Red Cloud's War." Following the battle, a peace commission met with the Plains tribes and agreed to assign specific territories to them. The U.S. also agreed to abandon its forts and forces from Lakota territory. In later life, Red Cloud became an important leader as the Lakotas transitioned from freedom to the confinement of the reservation system. He died still fighting for his people at the age of 87.

Photo: South Dakota State Historical Society. Public domain.

indication of Joseph's code is that Joseph was obedient to his father and persistent in seeking to carry out his father's assignment (see Genesis 37:12-17).

The fifth indication of Joseph's code is that "the LORD was with Joseph" in whatever Joseph did, so Joseph was able to make the best of every trouble with which he was confronted (Genesis 39:2,23). The sixth indication of Joseph's code is that although he had been forced into slavery, he served his master, Potiphar, with energy and integrity; and Potiphar trusted him implicitly (see Genesis 39:1-6). The seventh indication of Joseph's code is that he refused to commit adultery with Potiphar's wife and thus sin against God; instead, he ran away from temptation (see Genesis 39:7-15).

The eighth indication of Joseph's code is that when Joseph was unjustly confined in prison, he continued his habit of making the best of a terrible situation and using his gifts to make things better for those around him (see Genesis 39:20-23). This leads to the ninth indication of Joseph's code: When the cupbearer and the baker of Pharaoh displeased the king, he had them thrown into prison, where Joseph, noticing how very upset they both were, asked them about how they were doing.

JOSEPH'S FAITH IN GOD

The cupbearer and the baker had each had a troubling dream. Joseph told them, "Do not interpretations belong to God? Tell me your dreams" (Genesis 40:8). Joseph's words affirmed his steadfast faith in God, but at the same time he put his faith on the line by asking the two new prisoners to tell him their dreams so that he could interpret them. Joseph had a positive dream interpretation for the cupbearer: He would be restored to his former position. Once the cupbearer was back in his old position, Joseph asked him to remember Joseph and to talk the king into letting Joseph out of prison. The dream interpretation for the baker was not so rosy; Joseph told him he would be punished by death (see Genesis 40:18-19). Within three days, Joseph's interpretations of both dreams had been fulfilled. Unfortunately, the cupbearer forgot all about Joseph, and Joseph remained in the prison.

Two years later, Pharaoh had a couple of disturbing dreams that none of his wise men and magicians could interpret. At this point the cupbearer finally remembered Joseph, and the cupbearer told Pharaoh what Joseph had done for him in regard to his dreams. Joseph was then cleaned up and brought before the king. The king said to Joseph, "I have heard it said of you that when you hear a dream you can interpret it" (Genesis 41:15). Joseph's answer is yet another indication of his code of honor: Joseph said simply and boldly, "I cannot do it"—risking his own life—". . . but God will give Pharaoh the answer he desires"—again stepping out in faith (Genesis 41:16). Then Joseph told Pharaoh that his dreams meant that the next fourteen years would begin with seven years of plenty, followed by seven years of famine. Joseph then recommended that Pharaoh select an intelligent and insightful man to prepare for the bad times by stockpiling grain during the good years so that the Egyptians would be able to make it through the seven years of famine. Pharaoh said, "Can we find anyone like this man, one in whom is the spirit of God?" (Genesis 41:38).

So Pharaoh promoted Joseph to be his second in command and put on Joseph's finger a signet ring, a symbol of Pharaoh's authority. Pharaoh also gave Joseph an Egyptian name and an Egyptian wife.

Joseph carried out his plan to stockpile grain, and when the famine came, the Egyptians had more than enough food. In fact, people from other countries came to Egypt to buy grain from Joseph.

JESUS AS OUR MORAL COMPASS

Joseph's life gives us a theme that is picked up in various ways in other parts of the Bible. It's the theme that God is in the business of reversing terrible situations if we have faith in Him and Him alone.

God put Joseph through several severe trials, tested his character and his code of honor, and eventually promoted him from prison to a palace. In every challenge that Joseph faced, he never gave up his faith in God. And he knew that God's ways were the right ones, as evidenced especially by Joseph's reaction to Potiphar's wife. Joseph also acknowledged God as the source of his honorable behavior and his interpretation of dreams. Although Joseph's code of honor was man-made, it had been God inspired, and because God had not found Joseph's motives wanting, God had prospered Joseph.

Similarly, Jesus has done the same for us. Jesus freed us from the prison of sin and gave us the right to become royal children of God. He can turn around any horrendous problem or troubling situation we face and redeem it for His good purposes. He is in the process of lifting us from the dungeon of death and bringing us into eternal life. Jesus' life embodied the code of honor that we each should live by; it is Jesus' life that we should model. Even though our sinful nature means that we are not perfect, we should never give up trying to follow Jesus' code of conduct, because God is faithful. When we are tempted to sin, He will always provide a way for us to have victory over sin (see 1 Corinthians 10:13, our memory verse). No temptation, no trial, no misfortune of ours can defeat God's work in our lives. By His Spirit, He's going to be with us to endure whatever we face.

REFLECTION QUESTIONS

Why do you think it was so important for cowboys on the frontier to follow the Code of the West?

What spiritual truths can we derive from the Code of the West?

What are a few of the advantages of following a man-made code of honor?

What are a few of the weak points of any man-made code?

Read Philippians 2:1-8. Why is it appropriate for us to use Jesus as our model for how we act?

What are a few specific things about Jesus' behavior that we should model?

How is having Jesus as a moral compass related to resisting temptation and falling into sin?

Session Seven: Ultimate Moral Compass

Sometimes the outcomes of situations we face or we see others face may seem unjust. Based on the life of Jesus, the moral compass we should model, what should we do in such situations?

Read Hebrews 11. What two things did all the people described have in common?

Read John 3:15; 14:1-3. Why can we be so sure that God will deliver us from sin to eternal life?

What did Jesus do when Satan tempted Him in the desert (see Matthew 4:1-11; Luke 4:1-13)? What can you do when you're tempted to sin?

Notes

1. Pilar Wayne, *John Wayne: My Life with the Duke* (New York: McGraw-Hill Book Company, 1987), p. vii, quoted at *Wiki Answers*, 2012. http://wiki.answers.com/Q/Where_did_John_Wayne_say_a_man's_got_to_have_a_code_a_creed_to_live_by_no_matter_his_job (accessed July 2012).
2. Ramon F. Adams, *The Cowman and His Code of Ethics* (Austin, TX: Encino Press, 1969), quoted at "Old West Legends: The Code of the West," *Legends of America*, 2003-2012. http://www.legendsofamerica.com/we-codewest.html (accessed May 2012).
3. Kathy Etling, *The Quotable Cowboy*, Globe Pequot, 2005. http://books.google.com/books?id=4H5GLkQrmn0C&printsec=frontcover&dq=quotable+cowboy&hl=en&sa=X&ei=Lw7BUKOHGcna2QW00YCgDw&ved=0CDgQ6AEwAA#v=onepage&q=care&f=false (accessed July 2012).
4. Adams, *The Cowman and His Code of Ethics*.
5. Etling, *The Quotable Cowboy*, p. 53.
6. Ibid., p. 61.
7. Ibid., p. 27.
8. Theodore Roosevelt, *Hunting Trips of a Ranchman: Sketches of Sport on the Northern Cattle Plains* (New York: G. P. Putnam's Sons, 1885), quoted in Etling, *The Quotable Cowboy*, p. 52.
9. Clint Eastwood, foreword, in *Gathering Remnants: A Tribute to the Working Cowboy* (Sun Valley, ID: Prairie Creek Productions, 2001), quoted in Etling, *The Quotable Cowboy*, p. 49.

SESSION EIGHT

ULTIMATE ABUNDANCE

Genesis 42–47; 50:15-21

SESSION FOCUS

God provided abundantly for Joseph and enabled him to be a blessing to others. Jesus provided abundantly for us and wants us to be a blessing to others.

KEY VERSE

Seek first his kingdom and his righteousness, and all these things will be given to you as well that whoever believes in him shall not perish but have eternal life.

MATTHEW 6:33

SESSION AT A GLANCE

Section	60 Min.	90 Min.	What You Will Do
Getting started	10	15	Pray and worship
Main points of the chapter	25	35	Discuss the lonesome stranger motif in the Bible
Application and discussion	15	25	Discuss personal application questions
Looking ahead	5	5	Prepare for next week
Wrapping up	5	10	Close with prayer or song

God's abundance seemed to characterize the Old West. There were never-ending vistas, never-ending herds of animals, never-ending resources to tap. There seemed to be no limits on anything, and everything was available for the taking. Yes, the wealth of the Old West was available—be it land or cattle or gold—but a person had to be strong enough and smart enough to do the taking.

Keeping one's share of the abundance, though, was not guaranteed in the Old West. There were disputes over territory and mining claims, often settled by gunplay. There were constant dangers from wild animals and raiding parties. There were a lot of unscrupulous thieves who weren't above changing the brand on an animal or taking advantage of a newcomer.

Yes, the Old West was indeed a land of great abundance, but not all of the people who sought some if its wealth recognized or acknowledged the true source of the abundance.

ABUNDANCE FROM GOD

All abundance is, of course, from God: "Every good and perfect gift is from above, coming down from the Father of the heavenly lights, who does not change like shifting shadows" (James 1:17). God's supply of abundance is so great, in fact, that we can't even imagine its extent (see Ephesians 3:20).

And God is not stingy with His abundance. God provided for life itself to abundantly reproduce (see Genesis 1:11-13,20-29). God provided abundantly for His people in the wilderness (see Session 4). God promised that He would abundantly provide for His people in the Promised Land (see Deuteronomy 30:9). God offers us abundant life in Christ (see John 10:10) and wants to meet all our needs through Christ (see Philippians 4:19). He also wants to abundantly provide for us in His eternal kingdom (see Matthew 6:33; 2 Peter 1:11).

GOD'S ABUNDANCE TO JOSEPH

This generosity of God's abundance is illustrated in the biblical saga of Joseph. God had prospered Joseph, and Pharaoh had made Joseph second in command in Egypt, below only Pharaoh himself. Because of Joseph's wise decisions, the Egyptians did not suffer during the famine, as did peoples of other nations.

One of the nations that did suffer during the famine was Canaan, where Joseph's father and brothers were living. Eventually they were forced to send some of their number to Egypt to buy grain so that they could survive. When they finally arrived in Egypt, they bowed down to

Joseph, just as Joseph had foreseen in his dreams and told them about (see Genesis 37:5-10).

THE BROTHERS ARE TESTED

Joseph's brothers didn't recognize Joseph when they saw him in Egypt, but he recognized them. So Joseph asked them questions about their family and found out that he had a younger brother, Benjamin, who had been born after his brothers sold him into slavery. Then Joseph put them through a series of ruses to test them and see if they had learned anything over the years. He spoke harshly to them, accusing them of being spies. Then he demanded that they show their good faith that they weren't spies by leaving one of the brothers with him in Egypt and coming back with Benjamin, the youngest. Then, to strike even more fear in their hearts, he secretly had their silver returned to them in the sacks of grain he sold them, silver that they didn't discover until they were well on their journey home.

JACOB DESPAIRS

When the brothers (less Simeon) got home and told Jacob everything that had happened, Jacob spiraled into despair: "Joseph is no more and Simeon is no more, and now you want to take Benjamin. Everything is against me!" (Genesis 42:36). Rueben tried to calm his father and said he would guarantee the safety of Benjamin, but Jacob refused to let him go: "My son will not go down there with you; his brother is dead and he is the only one left. If harm comes to him on the journey you are taking, you will bring my gray head down to the grave in sorrow" (Genesis 42:38).

But the famine was severe. When the original grain that the family had purchased was almost gone, the brothers prevailed on their father to change his mind and let Benjamin come with them. Jacob was resigned: "May God Almighty give you mercy.... As for me, if I am bereaved, I am bereaved" (Genesis 43:14).

Then the brothers returned to Egypt to buy more grain. Joseph received them kindly this time, but he still didn't reveal himself. Rather, he put them through another test, this time not returning just their silver but also including his own silver cup. Then Joseph had his servants follow the brothers, open their sacks, find the silver and the cup, and accuse them of theft! When the brothers were brought before Joseph, they were really scared. But this time, Joseph had a surprise in store for them.

THE FAMILY IS RECONCILED

Joseph cleared the room and finally revealed himself for who he really was—their long-lost brother. They were stunned and speechless. Joseph told them to go get their father and bring him to Egypt, which they did. Then Pharaoh allowed them to settle in Goshen, "the best part of the land" (Genesis 47:11).

After Jacob died, Joseph's brothers began to worry that Joseph would now extract vengeance against them. "What if Joseph holds a grudge against us and pays us back for all the wrongs we did to him?" they said to each other (Genesis 50:15). So they sent word to Joseph and reminded him of their father's wish that he would forgive them for so badly treating him. Joseph wept and answered them with amazing words of forgiveness:

> Don't be afraid. Am I in the place of God? You intended to harm me, but God intended it for good to accomplish what is now being done, the saving of many lives. So then, don't be afraid. I will provide for you and your children (Genesis 50:19-21).

Joseph proved to be true to his word. He stayed in Egypt along with his brothers and all of Jacob's family. The Bible says he "lived a hundred and ten years and saw the third generation of Ephraim's children. . . . After they embalmed him, he was placed in a coffin in Egypt" (Genesis 50:22,26).

OLD WEST CHARACTERS

OLIVER WINCHESTER (1810–1880)

Oliver Winchester is best known for manufacturing the Winchester repeating rifle, known as the "Gun that Won the West" because of its predominant role in the hands of early American settlers. He began his career as a clothing manufacturer in New York City, but when he learned that a division of Smith & Wesson firearms was failing, he invested in the company. Despite slow initial sales, the company made refinements until the gun became the most popular rifle in the country. Winchester was also active in politics, serving as lieutenant governor of Connecticut in 1864. He died at the age of 70 in 1880.

Photo: Unknown. Public domain.

THE ONE THING WE NEED FROM GOD'S ABUNDANCE

According to the Bible, although all of God's abundance is available to us, we really only need *one thing*. The psalmist said, "*One thing* I have of the LORD, this is what I seek: that I may dwell in the house of the LORD all the days of my life, to gaze upon the beauty of the LORD and to seek him in his temple" (Psalm 27:4, emphasis added).

Jesus told Martha, who was upset because her sister, Mary, was not helping with dinner preparations: "Martha, Martha . . . you are worried and upset about many things, but only *one thing* is needed. Mary has chosen what is better, and it will not be taken away from her" (Luke 10:41-42, emphasis added).

Jesus said to the rich young ruler: "*One thing* you lack. . . . Go, sell everything you have and give to the poor, and you will have treasure in heaven. Then come, follow me" (Mark 10:21, emphasis added; see also Luke 18:22).

From this, we see that in the Bible, the *one thing we need* is not book knowledge. Rather, it is an experience, a person, a relationship. The blind man whom Jesus healed didn't know whether or not Jesus was a sinner, but he said, "*One thing* I do know. I was blind but now I see!" (John 9:25). The apostle Paul put it in slightly different words:

> When I came to you, I did not come with eloquence or human wisdom as I proclaimed to you the testimony about God. For I resolved to *know nothing* while I was with you except Jesus Christ and him crucified. I came to you in weakness with great fear and trembling. My message and my preaching were not with wise and persuasive words, but with a demonstration of the Spirit's power, so that your faith might not rest on human wisdom, but on God's power (1 Corinthians 2:1-5, emphasis added).

Later Paul said, "Brothers, I do not consider myself yet to have taken hold of it. But *one thing* I do: Forgetting what is behind and straining toward what is ahead, I press on toward the goal to win the prize for which God has called me heavenward in Christ Jesus. " (Philippians 3:13-14, emphasis added).

This *one thing* is what all of us want in the deepest part of our hearts—that part of us which is the image of God calling out to our Creator.

GOD'S ABUNDANCE THROUGH JESUS

Similar to what God did for Joseph, God wants to bless us with more than enough. For us, abundance comes through Jesus. As Jesus taught it, and as stated in our memory verse for this session: "Seek first [God's] kingdom and his righteousness, and all these things will be given to you as well" (Matthew 6:33).

Unfortunately, this *one thing*—God's kingdom, God's rule over every aspect of our lives—is something many of us tend to forget about at times. We get sidetracked and distracted by *so many things*. But what does "seek God's kingdom" mean? Are we supposed to be like a knight searching for some kind of Holy Grail or for a physical place where God's kingdom is supposed to materialize?

Joseph sought God's kingdom by being attentive to the movement of the Holy Spirit in his life, such as by noting dreams and being open to how God might be speaking through them. He made the best of each terrible situation in which he found himself and acted with integrity in every job given to him. He honored his relationships, such as by not degrading marriage by committing adultery with Potiphar's wife. He excercised the natural abilities and supernatural aptitudes that God had given him. He didn't allow himself to be consumed by thoughts of bitterness and revenge but practiced forgiveness with people who had desperately wronged him.

Joseph also looked out for others—especially in the way he looked after his family and the way he practised good management during the years of plenty so people in the region could survive in the bad years. As Genesis 41:47-49 states, "During the seven years of abundance the land produced plentifully. Joseph collected all the food produced in those seven years of abundance in Egypt and stored it in the cities. In each city he put the food grown in the fields surrounding it. Joseph stored up huge quantities of grain, like the sand of the sea; it was so much that he stopped keeping records because it was beyond measure." In summary, every day Joseph sought to glorify God with every day of life that God gave him.

Jesus said that what we are to do is what Joseph did: obey God and serve Him, turn to God when we have a problem, use God's behavior as our example to model, and thank God every day for whatever it is that we have. All of this comes as a response to the God of life—the God of goodness and the giver of good gifts. He is the God of love who gives us the ability to love Him back.

REFLECTION QUESTIONS

We hear a lot about abundance and its opposite—scarcity—in the world today. What do you think about how the abundance of natural resources, for example, is handled in America? In the world?

Do you feel as if your life is overflowing with abundance or do you feel the pinch of scarcity? Why do you feel the way that you do?

What are some of the ways that Joseph experienced God's abundance?

Read Genesis 46:1-4. What promise did God make to Jacob on Jacob's way to Egypt? Why would God's words to him have been comforting?

What are some of the ways that Joseph's father and brothers experienced God's abundance?

How can you position yourself to tap into God's abundance and receive His blessings?

How does a person know if what he or she is experiencing is God's blessing or some scheme by Satan to ensnare the person?

What kinds of things do people do that cut them off from God's abundance or minimize God's blessings?

What are a few specific ways that a person can "seek first [God's] kingdom and his righteousness" (Matthew 6:33)?

What do you think Jesus meant by "all these things" (Matthew 6:33)?

SESSION NINE

ULTIMATE REDEMPTION

Psalms 66; 105:12-41

SESSION FOCUS

God revealed His will and intentions in the Old Testament. Jesus, revealed in the New Testament, fulfilled God's will and intention to redeem us.

KEY VERSE

Blessed is the man who perseveres under trial, because he has stood the test, he will receive the crown of life that God has promised to those who love him.

JAMES 1:12

SESSION AT A GLANCE

Section	60 Min.	90 Min.	What You Will Do
Getting started	10	15	Pray and worship
Main points of the chapter	25	35	Discuss salvation and redemption and how these relate to remembrance, works and rewards
Application and discussion	15	25	Discuss personal application questions
Looking ahead	5	5	Prepare for next week
Wrapping up	5	10	Close with prayer or song

The hero in a Western, like the hero in many dramas, often has a dubious past. Although the reader or movie watcher may know something about this past, and the people with whom the hero interacts may suspect that something is odd or unusual about the hero, they are unaware of the exact nature of the hero's past.

REDEMPTION IN WESTERNS

The storyline in many Westerns follows a pattern of introducing a hero who appears to be more than what you see. There always seems to be some aspect of the hero's past that he doesn't want to talk about and doesn't want to reveal in any way. Then the hero is put into a trying circumstance and is severely tested to see what his or her true nature is. The test itself often involves risking everything the person values, including his love or life. The character must choose between love and duty, cowardice and courage. It is said of those who pass these tests that they "find redemption" or that they "redeem themselves." You don't find these characters passively waiting for God to act; they redeem themselves by their own actions.

Such is the case with the character of, for example, Shane (in the novel or movie of the same name). Shane does not reveal his past, but one suspects that it has something to do with the use of a gun. He tries to settle down peaceably with a homesteading family, but he is soon drawn into a local conflict. Put to the test, he resolves the situation by using his gun—to do good: He saves the homesteader and redeems whatever he did in the past.

In the film *Rio Bravo,* the storyline includes a sheriff's deputy who must redeem himself from his reputation as a drunk who will do anything for a drink.

In the television show *Alias Smith and Jones,* both of the main characters try to redeem their past lives of crime by turning their lives around.

Where does God fit in to this sort of drama? Can this sort of redemption be reconciled with biblical truth? The answer is neither completely no nor completely yes.

GOD'S REVELATION OF REDEMPTION

To arrive at a biblical answer, we need to think about the biblical understanding of salvation and redemption from the perspective of both the Old and the New Testaments. And to understand that, we need to realize that the Bible is a record of God's dealing with humanity that gradually unfolds into a more and more complete perspective. The Bible is a progressive revelation of God's will and intentions.

God did not reveal everything about His plans all at once. Rather, He revealed things to people little by little, and in doing so He accommodated Himself to the cultural level of people's understanding at the time. The Old Testament is Bible history and teaching *before* Jesus; the New Testament is Bible history and teaching *about and after* the coming of Jesus. By recording prophecy, using foreshadowing and giving literary clues, the Old Testament tells us about the future coming of a Messiah. But the fuller manifestation of the Messiah—who He is and what He stands for—is not spelled out until the coming of Jesus, which is described in the New Testament.

This way that God has revealed His will and intentions has confused some Christians. They read about all the hundreds of laws of Moses in the Old Testament and conclude that during the time of the Old Testament, people saved themselves by means of their good deeds and good character and by meticulously following the letter of the Mosaic law. This very confused idea of what the Old Testament teaches is often combined with the idea that only the New Testament teaches that people are saved by grace. Unfortunately, this teaching neglects key Old Testament teaching about God's grace redeeming people and making them righteous in God's sight (see for example Genesis 15:6: "Abram believed the LORD, and he credited it to him as righteousness"). Also, this confused idea forgets prophecies about how the Messiah would suffer in our place (see for example Isaiah 53). God planned that the Messiah would come to die for the sins of the whole world, but that does not negate the fact that redemption and salvation are described in both Testaments as being available by God's grace, through faith.

THE CONCEPTS OF SALVATION AND REDEMPTION

The concepts of redemption and salvation themselves develop into a brighter and brighter vision in the Bible as we move deeper and deeper into God's progressive revelation.

IN THE OLD TESTAMENT
In the Old Testament, salvation most often points in a horizontal, this-worldly direction. People are saved from certain disaster, from sickness,

from evil men or from slavery and oppression. People are redeemed for God-glorifying purposes. Salvation and redemption are not primarily distant, futuristic, other-worldly, floating-on-clouds-and-playing-harps kinds of things. They are concepts and hopes grounded in the belief that God can intervene—and has intervened decisively—in real-world, this-life crises. God has changed the course of human events.

We see this fervent hope in God-who-intervenes in David's Psalm 27. David is not afraid, even though his enemies seek to destroy him. He does not pin his hope on the future; rather, he says, "I am still confident of this: I will see the goodness of the LORD in the land of the living" (Psalm 27:13).

Therefore the psalmist waits, not with resignation that his only real hope is in an afterlife, but with anticipation that God can change things in the here and now. We can, therefore, do the same. It is not only permissible, but it is also good and right to hope for better circumstances that God may bring about now and in our present circumstances.

Our only hope of change is not just in eternity. And because of that fact, it is good and prudent to prepare ourselves, by faith, to take advantage of those changes when they occur. This kind of preparation can take many forms, including giving thanks ahead of time for what God will do (see Psalm 50:23), praying, sharpening our skills, meeting with other Christians, and planning for the future.

OLD WEST CHARACTERS

WONG KIM ARK (BORN c. 1871)

The growth of the railroad industry in the Old West led many companies to hire workers from China, who were often given the dangerous blasting work. By the late 1800s, many Chinese immigrants had settled in San Francisco. One such individual, named Wong Kim Ark, visited China in 1894 and, on returning home, was denied readmittance because he was not deemed a citizen. He sued in court, and eventually his case was heard before the U.S. Supreme Court. In a landmark decision, the court ruled that a person born in the U.S. was a legal U.S. citizen, regardless of whether his or her parents were citizens.

Photo: National Archives and Records Administration. Public domain.

We would be dreadfully mistaken to think that the Old Testament hope for salvation is reserved strictly for this world or that the Old Testament lacks hope in an afterlife. On the contrary, the Old Testament provides many hints and affirmations of an afterlife (see, for example, 2 Kings 2:1,11; Job 19:25-27; Psalms 16:9-11; 23:6; Isaiah 66:24; Daniel 12:2-3). Belief in the afterlife is not absent in the Old Testament; it's just not as fully developed or emphasized as in the New Testament.

IN THE NEW TESTAMENT

If the afterlife is in the background in the Old Testament, it is in the foreground in the New Testament. In the New Testament, justification (being made right with God, or being made righteous before God) and eternal life (everlasting acceptance and participation with God in the afterlife) are two central concerns. Sin pollutes us and makes us unfit for heaven; but when we confess our sins and repent, Jesus cleanses us from sin and opens the doors of heaven for us.

But salvation and redemption in the New Testament are not just pie in the sky. We are saved for specific purposes:

> For it is by grace you have been saved, through faith—and this not from yourselves, it is the gift of God—not by works, so that no one can boast. We are God's workmanship, created in Christ Jesus to do good works, which God prepared in advance for us to do (Ephesians 2:8-10).

We are redeemed, not because of our good works, but once we are redeemed, our lives are changed, and good works are the evidence of that change. Paul even told the people in one early church that, because they had now been saved, he expected them to do good works—in particular to be his partners in spreading the gospel—and he expected God to be fully engaged in the process:

> I thank my God every time I remember you. In all my prayers for all of you, I always pray with joy because of your partnership in the gospel from the first day until now, being confident of this, that he who began a good work in you will carry it on to completion until the day of Christ Jesus. It is right for me to feel this way about all of you, since I have you in my heart (Philippians 1:3-7).

Working out our faith through deeds is a good part of the history of the Church. Christians have often been at the forefront of ministries such as feeding the hungry; or taking care of the sick, the widows and the orphans; or visiting and encouraging those who are imprisoned; or spurring forward various movements for social justice (such as the abolition of slavery and the establishment of skid-row missions and peace-and-reconciliation ministries, among others). Our ultimate hope is in heaven, but in the meantime, just like the believers in the Old Testament, we place our hope in God to alter the situation down here "on earth as it is in heaven" (Matthew 6:10).

To fulfill our calling, however, means overcoming our own inertia and laziness, overcoming the skepticism of friends and family—overcoming people and attitudes and circumstances that want to put us down or defeat us—and, as our memory verse reminds us, that means we're going to need a lot of perseverance (James 1:12). But when we persevere, we will be delivered.

REMEMBRANCE OF BEING DELIVERED

In the Bible, remembrance is not just remembering or recalling to mind; it is an act of re-enacting or reliving the actions of God in history. It is also about believing that because God fulfilled His promises in the past, He will do so in the future. And remembrance of all that God has done naturally leads to praising God for His faithful deliverance.

We see this attitude in Psalm 66. Here the psalmist calls for not only all of the people but also all of creation to see and acknowledge what God has done. But the psalmist also reviews history, in particular that God delivered His people, saving them at the Red Sea. The author likens God's saving of him to God's past act and as another fulfillment of God's promise to hear prayers and answer them.

The psalmist also recognizes that times of trouble are God's way of testing people and removing impurities from them to make them more like Him. Because the psalmist loved and obeyed God, God had listened to his prayer.

Psalm 105:12-41 also calls for the remembrance of God's saving acts. The psalmist suggests that we should trust God because God fulfilled His promises in the past, recalling the Exodus and God's fulfillment of His covenant with Abraham.

OUR REDEMPTION BY JESUS

We can follow the example of God's people in the past who by faith trusted God, overcame obstacles and obtained the promises God made to them. And Christ fulfilled one of the earliest of God's promises recorded in the Bible:

> Cursed are you [the serpent] above all the livestock and all the wild animals! You will crawl on your belly and you will eat dust all the days of your life. And I will put enmity between you and the woman, and between your offspring and hers; he will crush your head, and you will strike his heel (Genesis 3:14-15).

God promised that He would send a Savior who would overcome Adam's sin; and even though Jesus was tempted by Satan, He remained perfect, making Him the only One who could take the punishment for our sins. In the end, Jesus will have victory over Satan, symbolized by the snake, and we too will be raised from the dead:

> Christ has indeed been raised from the dead, the firstfruits of those who have fallen asleep. For since death came through a man, the resurrection of the dead comes also through a man. For as in Adam all die, so in Christ all will be made alive. But each in his own turn: Christ, the firstfruits; then, when he comes, those who belong to him (1 Corinthians 15:20-23).

Because Jesus died and rose again, we have proof that we too will be raised from the dead. There is no guarantee of any sort of earthly reward for following Jesus. Sometimes doing good and following Jesus have to be their own reward, and the "crown" will be deferred. We may even have to suffer in silence, persevering through the problems and troubles that confront us in life. As Jesus told His disciples:

> I have told you these things, so that in me you may have peace. In this world you will have trouble. But take heart! I have overcome the world (John 16:33).

However, during such times we can always remember that God promises a coming day when we will receive "the crown of life" (James 1:12). And what a day of rejoicing that will be!

REFLECTION QUESTIONS

In the old West, from a human standpoint, under what circumstances might a person seek to redeem himself or herself? How do people try to do this today?

What's the problem with saying that we can redeem ourselves before God (see Ephesians 2:8-9)?

What is the main focus of salvation and redemption in the Old Testament?

What is the main focus of salvation and redemption in the New Testament?

Session Nine: Ultimate Redemption

What does the Old Testament teach about the afterlife (see 2 Kings 2:1,11; Job 19:25-27; Psalms 16:9-11; 23:6; Isaiah 66:24; Daniel 12:2-3)?

Many people say the New Testament is only interested in "pie in the sky when you die." What does the New Testament teach about being involved in this-world concerns (see Ephesians 2:10; Philippians 1:4-6; James 1:27)?

Why is remembrance important in regard to salvation and redemption (see Deuteronomy 26:1-6; Psalms 66; 105)?

In what ways are deeds, or works, important in regard to salvation and redemption?

In what ways do Christians practice remembrance for what Christ has done for us?

Why or why is it not okay for Christians to think about and encourage each other regarding rewards, including heaven?

SESSION TEN

ULTIMATE ALLEGIANCE

Deuteronomy 4

SESSION FOCUS

God protected His Chosen People and wanted them to obey only Him. Jesus will always protect those who follow and obey Him.

KEY VERSES

My sheep listen to my voice; I know them, and they follow me. I give them eternal life, and they shall never perish; no one can snatch them out of my hand.

JOHN 10:27-28

SESSION AT A GLANCE

Section	60 Min.	90 Min.	What You Will Do
Getting started	10	15	Pray and worship
Main points of the chapter	25	35	Discuss how God "brands" us and speaks to us as His own
Application and discussion	15	25	Discuss personal application questions
Looking ahead	5	5	Prepare for next week
Wrapping up	5	10	Close with prayer or song

It is said that a good cowboy is "loyal to his brand." He "pledges allegiance" to the ranch for which he works, symbolized by the brand that that ranch uses to identify the ownership of its animals. A cowboy also knows the brands of all the local ranches.

BRANDING IN THE OLD WEST

The practice of using a brand—of branding—started in ancient times and refers to marking ownership of animals with something hot. In the Old West, a piece of iron with the symbol representing a particular rancher would be heated until red-hot and then pressed into the hide of a cow (or a horse). The resultant scar marked that cow as belonging to a particular herd.

Branding was particularly important in the early days of open ranges in the Old West when cattle from different ranches grazed together freely. When it came time for the ranchers to gather their particular animals, the brand would identify which animals belonged to each ranch owner. Branding also made it easier to track and to return lost cows to their rightful owners. Cattle rustlers often tried to change a brand in order to steal cattle, but such alterations were not always successful.

The trick in branding was to come up with a brand that was distinct and that no unscrupulous person could over-brand, counterfeiting the original brand. If you study the brands of a particular area, you will notice endless ingenuity, creativity and artistry in the brands. Here are some examples of brands from familes in eastern Oregon around the turn of the century.[1]

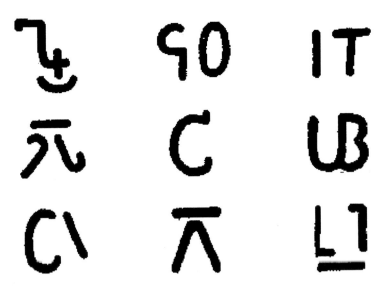

Although talk about brands and branding today is most often heard among people in marketing and advertising, branding of animals is still practiced in the livestock industry.

BRANDING AT SINAI

Although there is no literal branding mentioned in the Bible, there is a metaphorical branding described in Deuteronomy 4–5.

Repetition of the Law

The setting for the book of Deuteronomy is just east of the Jordan River across from Canaan. The Israelites were on the verge of entering the Promised Land, and the book of Deuteronomy itself is a recap of what God had done for the Israelites in the past and a foretaste of what God wanted to do for them in the near future. "Deuteronomy" literally means "repetition of the law," something of which the Israelites were in need.

The Debacle at Peor

First, through Moses, God reminded the people of the debacle at Peor, when Israelite men were seduced to participate in sexual immorality and to worship other gods (see Deuteronomy 4:3-4; Numbers 25:1-9). The Moabites and Midianites, perceiving the Israelites to be a threat, had hired Balaam, a prophet-for-hire, to curse them. Balaam was about to pronounce his curse when God instead caused him to bless the Israelites—not once, but three times (see Numbers 22–24). But by the time of the last blessing, the Israelites had lapsed into sin. The men began to indulge in sexual immorality with the Moabite women, and the people began worshiping other gods rather than the Lord (see Numbers 25).

The Worldview of Polytheism

At this point we need to pause for a moment and think about the worldview that prevailed among the peoples of the time who surrounded the Israelites. That worldview was polytheism: the belief that many gods controlled, or influenced, natural events—everything from mountain building to streams flowing, from storms to sunlight, from war to peace. Every aspect of life was subject to one god (or spirit) or another.

In addition to the main gods, there also were goddesses—wives or consorts of the gods. Among the gods and goddesses, there were dysfunctional family relationships—including adultery and sibling rivalries—that resulted in bad blood between the gods and goddesses. Humans were seen as being pretty much at the mercy of these unseen powers. The purpose of religion, then, was to appease and if possible placate capricious gods so that they would do what people wanted them to do.

At odds with the belief in many gods came the word of Yahweh to the Israelites, the acts of Yahweh on behalf of the Israelites, and the rule of law and justice that guided the Israelites. The surrounding nations were supposed to sit up and take notice, admiring the wisdom and understanding of the Israelites. And the Israelites were supposed to notice that the other nations' gods were not near their people the way the Lord was to the Israelites (see Deuteronomy 4:5-8).

This is why there was more than one strong reminder of everything the Lord had done for the Israelites (see Deuteronomy 4:9-14,32-34) and why there was a strong warning against the Israelites taking upon themselves any form of idolatry as they moved into the Promised Land (see Deuteronomy 4:15-20). The sin that had caused such problems at Peor must be avoided at all costs.

Our God of Anger and Jealousy

Moses then told the Israelites, "The LORD was angry with me because of you," and that because of that, he would not be going into the Promised Land with them (Deuteronomy 4:21). Moses used his own sin as a connection between himself and the Israelites to emphasize the importance of obedience and the result of sinning. Then Moses issued another warning against idolatry: "For the LORD your God is a consuming fire, a jealous God" (Deuteronomy 4:24). Idolatry is evil and arouses the Lord's anger;

Old West Characters
Laura Ingalls Wilder (1867–1957)

Laura Ingalls Wilder was an American author who is best known for her *Little House on the Prairie* series of books. She was born in the "Big Woods" of Wisconsin and grew up on the prairies of what is now Independence, Kansas. She began teaching at the age of 16 to help support her family, but quit two years later when she married Almanzo Wilder, who was 10 years her senior. Inspired by her daughter, Rose, she began writing in 1911 and landed a position as a columnist for a local paper. She published *Little House in the Big Woods* in 1931, which lauched her career as a writer. She died in 1957 at the age of 90.

Photo: Unkonwn. Public domain.

and the people were warned that if they corrupted themselves with idolatry, they would be destroyed as a nation, and what was left of them would be scattered among the nations.

We must not think that God's anger is like human anger or that His jealousy is like human jealousy. God's anger is based upon holiness, justice and what is right; human anger is based upon having our wants and desires blocked. God's jealousy is based upon His getting the praise He deserves; human jealousy is based upon us wanting what we know is rightfully someone else's. The Lord's ways are tough, but they are to be conscientiously followed. Having sinful natures, we unfortunately often find ourselves on the wrong path. But the Lord always leaves His people a way out of their misery and a way back to Him:

> If from there you seek the LORD your God, you will find him if you look for him with all your heart and with all your soul. When you are in distress and all these things have happened to you, then in later days you will return to the LORD your God and obey him. For the LORD your God is a merciful God; he will not abandon or destroy you or forget the covenant with your forefathers, which he confirmed to them by oath (Deuteronomy 4:29-31).

When we renew our allegiance to God and recommit ourselves to Him, He will be merciful to us.

God's Branding of His People

The Lord had spoken out of the fire, He had performed miracles, and He had brought the Israelites out of Egypt. As Moses said to the people:

> Has any god ever tried to take for himself one nation out of another nation, by testings, by miraculous signs and wonders, by war, by a mighty hand and an outstretched arm, or by great and awesome deeds, like all the things the LORD your God did for you in Egypt before your very eyes? You were shown these things so that you might know that the LORD is God; besides him there is no other" (Deuteronomy 4:35).

God was now about to drive out nations stronger and more powerful than they; He was about to establish them in the Promised Land. The Lord, and the Lord alone, deserved the credit, the honor, the admiration, and the worship (see Deuteronomy 4:36-40). God had branded His people as His. They were to follow the Ten Commandments and always remember to whom they belonged.

A NEW KIND OF BRANDING THROUGH THE BLOOD OF JESUS

We, too, have been branded—with the blood of Christ—and we should listen to the One to whom we belong. His scars have become ours; they have cleansed us and forgiven our sins. Christ's sacrifice has ransomed us and redeemed us for God's good purposes. Should that branding not purchase some loyalty from us?

Cowboys tell about how they come to know the cattle, and the cattle come to know them. Sometimes at night, the cattle get restless. When that happens, a cowboy needs to ride out and talk to the herd; when the cows hear the cowboy's familiar voice, they settle down. Similarly, Jesus' voice offers His followers the security we need to be at peace:

> The watchman opens the gate for him, and the sheep listen to his voice. He calls his own sheep by name and leads them out. When he has brought out all his own, he goes on ahead of them, and his sheep follow him because they know his voice. . . . I am the good shepherd; I know my sheep and my sheep know me—just as the Father knows me and I know the Father—and I lay down my life for the sheep. I have other sheep that are not of this sheep pen. I must bring them also. They too will listen to my voice, and there shall be one flock and one shepherd. . . . My sheep listen to my voice; I know them, and they follow me. I give them eternal life, and they shall never perish; no one will snatch them out of my hand (John 10:3-4,14-16,27-28).

We may have earthly problems and troubles, but Jesus will always care for us and protect us, just like a shepherd watches out for his flock of sheep. It is the privilege of the believer to hear Jesus' voice, the prompting of the Holy Spirit, the voice from heaven. We daily must recommit our allegiance to the brand we carry: Jesus.

REFLECTION QUESTIONS

Why was branding an important aspect of ranching in the Old West?

How did God show He had "branded" the Israelites as His own "property" (see Deuteronomy 4:1,6)?

Why was it important that the Israelites "not add to" what God commanded them to do (Deuteronomy 4:2)?

How were the Israelites to show they had wisdom (see Deuteronomy 4:6)?

Are all of God's laws—including but not limited to the Ten Commandments—applicable to God's people today?

Why does idolatry cause God to become extremely angry and jealous?

What types of idolatry do some people practice in today's world?

Why should we turn to God when we sin or have feelings of despair (see Deuteronomy 4:29-31)?

Session Ten: Ultimate Allegiance

Read John 10:27-30. Why can we feel so secure about the ability of our Shepherd to protect us?

In what specific ways does the world know that you have been branded by Jesus and that your allegiance is only to Him?

Note

1. Depictions of brands listed in Herman Oliver, *Gold and Cattle Country* (Hillsboro, OR: Binford & Mort Publishing, 1967), p. 9-4.

SESSION ELEVEN

ULTIMATE LEGACY

Deuteronomy 6

SESSION FOCUS

God told parents to teach their children to love and obey Him. Jesus will help every generation to love and obey Him.

KEY VERSES

Hear, O Israel: The LORD our God, the LORD is one. Love the LORD your God with all your heart and with all your soul and with all your strength. These commandments that I give you today are to be upon your hearts. Impress them on your children. Talk about them when you sit at home and when you walk along the road, when you lie down and when you get up

DEUTERONOMY 6:4-7

SESSION AT A GLANCE

Section	60 Min.	90 Min.	What You Will Do
Getting started	10	15	Pray and worship
Main points of the chapter	25	35	Discuss what is entailed in passing on a legacy of faith to future generations
Application and discussion	15	25	Discuss personal application questions
Looking ahead	5	5	Prepare for next week
Wrapping up	5	10	Close with prayer or song

Aside from the written accounts we have of the Old West, we also have artwork from the period. So even if we questioned or doubted the written description of something from the past, we have paintings or photographs made by people who were there. We have a legacy of artwork.

A LEGACY OF ARTWORK FROM THE OLD WEST

The most famous artists who chronicled the Old West include George Catlin, Alfred Bierstadt, Thomas Moran, William Henry Jackson, Frederic Remington, Charles Marion Russell, and Edward S. Curtis. All of them knew they were memorializing a West that soon would be no more. They were visual poets of a mythic, vanishing age.

Beginning in 1830 and continuing until about 1838, George Catlin travelled in Native American territory from Florida to the Great Lakes to the Great Plains and North Dakota. Along the way, he visited more than 50 tribes, collecting artifacts and painting a wide-range of personalities and ways of life. Caitlin was known well enough among both whites and Native Americans that despite skirmishes and warfare between the two, the Native Americans granted Catlin safe passage in their territories.[1]

Alfred Bierstadt, a German by birth, became famous for painting large, romantic landscapes of the American West, which he began producing in 1860. Among his works are paintings of what would become Yellowstone and Yosemite National Parks. Although he sometimes exaggerated details or added things to some of his landscape paintings, he helped Easterners value the magnificence of the untrammeled, undeveloped West.[2]

Thomas Moran was an English-born American landscape painter and printmaker. His images of the American West of the 1870s, particularly those of the Yellowstone region, helped persuade lawmakers to make Yellowstone a national park in 1872.[3]

Photographs made by William Henry Jackson also helped persuade the lawmakers to make Yellowstone a national park. Jackson also became well known for his photographs of other landmarks and his many images taken for the railroads along possible future routes.[4]

Frederic Remington, a New Yorker who began working as an artist in the 1880s, immortalized the Old West in his detailed paintings, etchings, illustrations and sculptures. On his trips out West, he collected artifacts that he later used as props in his work, and he is particularly noted for the authenticity of the colors that he used in his images, because they were based on his actual observations.[5]

Charles Marion Russell was both a real cowboy and a self-taught artist who drew, painted and sculpted. His vigorous, action-packed work portrays cowboys, Indians, cavalry units, and landscapes inspired by his travels and life out west in the late 1800s and early 1900s.[6]

Edward S. Curtis was one of the most important photographers of the American West and of its Native American peoples, which he began photographing in the 1890s and continued working with into the early 1900s. Curtis not only photographed his subjects, but he also wrote about them; and some of his historical work is the only record we have of some people.[7]

Each of the artists of the Old West probably hoped—as any artist with a long vision hopes—that he or she would speak, not just to the immediate generation, who could view the artwork while the artist was alive, but also to future generations, who would also be able to experience the artwork.

A LEGACY OF FAITH IN THE OLD TESTAMENT

The motive of an artist is somewhat different from what Moses had in mind when he reminded the Israelites about their God and what He expected from them. Moses wanted to pass on to future generations a legacy of faith.

Moses had spent 40 years in Egypt as a child of privilege, 40 years in the desert herding sheep and 40 years as the leader of the Israelites on the move in the desert. Recorded in the book of Deuteronomy are Moses' closing words to the Chosen People, getting them ready to make do without him. He had the serious job of reminding them how they had gotten to where they were now and what they should expect in the future.

History

Moses got right to the point, reminding the present generation of the history of God's Chosen People (see Deuteronomy 1–4) and reiterating the Ten Commandments (see Deuteronomy 5). This was particularly important because the generation to whom Moses spoke was not the generation he had led out of Egypt. That generation, except for Joshua and Caleb, had died in the desert. Moses was now standing in front of the younger generation, the generation that had seen their parents die because of their lack of faith. A crucial transition had to be made, and these second-generation people had to be aware of what had happened in the past, because it would affect their future; and everyone had to be in agreement about what to do in the new land.

The Charge

Moses' objective was to solidify agreement by getting commitment. And he first pointed out that the commandments and laws he had spoken of were laws from God that they were to put into effect in Canaan, the Promised Land they were about to enter. By obeying God's laws, the present generation and all the generations to come would be blessed by God (see Deuteronomy 6:1-3). God's promise to Abraham was now the promise for the current generation and for future generations.

The Shema

Moses then told the people what has come to be known as the central theme of Deuteronomy, the Shema, which has also become known as the Jewish confession of faith (see Deuteronomy 6:4-9). It is named after the first Hebrew word of the passage, *shema, or* "hear," and it is a pivotal part of Jewish prayer life:

> The Shema is the central prayer in the Jewish prayerbook (Siddur) and is often the first section of Scripture that a Jewish child learns. During its recitation in the synagogue, Orthodox Jews pronounce each word very carefully and cover their eyes with their right hand. Many Jews recite the Shema at least twice daily: once in the morning and once in the evening.[8]

Old West Characters
Frederic Remington (1861–1909)

Frederic Remington was a painter and sculptor who specialized in creating depictions from the Old West. He first became interested in drawing such scenes at the age of 19 when he took a camping trip to Montana. In 1887, he was asked to do 83 illustrations for a book by Theodore Roosevelt, which sparked a long-term friendship. He was frequently sent on assignment to cover U.S. troop actions in the Old West, where he would paint portraits of Army officers. By the time of his death, his fame had grown to such an extent that other Western painters were known as being in the "School of Remington."

Photo: Davis and Sanford (1909). Public domain.

Hear, O Israel: The LORD our God, the LORD is one—Moses told the people that their first duty was to witness to themselves and the surrounding nations that the Lord was their God and that the Lord was one. This declaration was vital for the Israelites to acknowledge, because the people in the land they were about to enter worshiped many gods. The belief in the one true God would further distinguish God's Chosen People from the peoples that they would displace.

It should be noted that the original Hebrew word for "one" is *echad*, which can mean "absolute singularity" (or "one and only one"), but it can also imply "unity within diversity." This point is extremely important, because when you look at the entire biblical revelation from Genesis to Revelation, it is clear that the one eternal Creator-God has always existed as God the Father, God the Son, and God the Holy Spirit. Nothing in the teaching of the Trinity contradicts the Shema.

Love the LORD your God with all your heart and with all your soul and with all your strength—The heart of biblical faith is God's love eliciting our love back to Him. And our love should be given with our whole being.

These commandments that I give you today are to be upon your hearts—God's commandments are to be such an integral part of our lives that we cannot be separated from them.

Impress them on your children—Religious education should be an integral part of every child's life. And that education should start in the home, beginning with education from the parents.

Talk about them when you sit at home and when you walk along the road, when you lie down and when you get up—God's laws are to be part of everyday life. Children daily need to see their parents living out God's laws and to hear their parents speak about the laws, not just practice them during specific religious events or ceremonies. Children need to see faith in action.

Tie them as symbols on your hands and bind them on your foreheads—God's laws are to be so ingrained that it should seem as if they are literally tied to your hands and heads. (Orthodox Jews take this literally, tying phylacteries to their arms and foreheads.)

Write them on the doorframes of your houses and on your gates—God's laws are also to mark the homes of those who believe in Him. This marks the homes and the people who live within them as belonging to God. (In many Jewish homes today, the Shema is written on a small piece of parchment [mezuzah], rolled up, placed inside a small container and affixed to the entryway and/or every doorframe of every room in the home.) The point was to give the ancient Israelites, and their children, physical reminders of spiritual truths. And the point of that is that one's physical life is a big part of one's spiritual life: The spiritual life is not only about intangibles but also about here-and-now realities.

Relationship

Moses then spoke about how the people were to have a right relationship with God. And the first thing the people were to do was remember all that God had done for them. People must never forget that it was God working on their behalf that freed them from slavery. Nothing that had been achieved had been solely through human efforts.

By loving God, by having a healthy respect for Him and by obeying Him, all would go well for the people. And the people were to pass on to their children the legacy of faith.

A LEGACY FROM JESUS

Jesus and His contemporaries probably recited the Shema, and Jesus even quoted part of it as *the* most important commandment (see Matthew 22:37-38; Mark 12:29-30; Luke 10:27).

It is significant that Mark and Luke wrote that Jesus added a little twist to this verse when He added the phrase "and with all your mind." As much as loving God is about the heart, the soul and the will, it is also about respecting the mind—the process of thinking and using your intellect as much as you can to glorify Him. Jesus was basically telling His disciples, "Do not neglect the gift of the mind!"

But, if we're honest, there's a problem: While there are good places in our souls, wills and minds, there are also dark places. To compound matters, we too often repress or deny that truth. We too often allow ourselves to be selfish, get unrighteously angry or become depressed. We make excuses and blame others for our bad actions. How can we human beings really love God?

Christians must look to the legacy Jesus gave us, and to do that, we must look to the cross. At the cross is God's irrevocable demonstration of His love for broken humanity and for each of us personally: "God so loved the world that He gave His one and only Son" (John 3:16). "We love because He first loved us" (1 John 4:19). The cross had not yet happened for Moses and ancient Israel; they had a glimpse of God's love. For us looking back, we have a much fuller revelation of God's love for us, for which we should be very thankful.

Jesus, the fulfillment of God's love for us, made it clear that He loves us just as His Father loves Him, and the way we show our love is to obey God's commands, just as Jesus did (see John 15:9-17). We are to follow in the footsteps of Jesus, continuing the legacy of love and faith.

REFLECTION QUESTIONS

How does artwork of the Old West operate for us as a true legacy of that time period? How does it operate as a false legacy?

Why is the repetition of what God has done for His people so important to a legacy of faith?

Why or why do you not think that the Shema is an accurate confession of faith?

How do you explain that the one eternal Creator-God has always existed as God the Father, God the Son, and God the Holy Spirit?

What kinds of things keep us from loving God with our whole hearts?

Briefly describe any physical reminders (such as signs, plaques, pictures, crosses) about God, His commandments or His faithfulness that you have in your home, on your person or in your car. Also tell why each of these things is important to you.

Session Eleven: Ultimate Legacy

Whether you have physical reminders or not, why are such things good to have? Why might they be bad?

_____
_____
_____
_____
_____
_____

Why do you think that Jesus added the phrase "and with all your mind" to the Shema?

_____
_____
_____
_____
_____
_____

In what ways did Jesus leave us a legacy of faith?

_____
_____
_____
_____
_____
_____
_____

What are a few specific things you can do to leave a legacy of faith if you have children?

How can you leave a legacy of faith even if you do not have any children?

Notes
1. "George Catlin," Wikipedia. http://en.wikipedia.org/wiki/George_Catlin.
2. "Albert Bierstadt," Wikipedia. http://en.wikipedia.org/wiki/Albert_Bierstadt.
3. "Thomas Moran," Wikipedia. http://en.wikipedia.org/wiki/Thomas_Moran.
4. "William Henry Jackson," Wikipedia. http://en.wikipedia.org/wiki/William_Henry_Jackson.
5. "Frederic Remington," Wikipedia. http://en.wikipedia.org/wiki/Frederic_Remington.
6. "Famous American Western Artists: Remington, Russell, Catlin, Bierstadt, Moran," HubPages. http://wannabwestern.hubpages.com/hub/10-Western-Artists.
7. "Edward S. Curtis," Wikipedia. http://en.wikipedia.org/wiki/Edward_S._Curtis.
8. "The Shema—Hear, O Israel!" *Hebrew for Christians,* John J. Parsons. http://www.hebrew4christians.com/Scripture/Torah/The_Shema/the_shema.html.

SESSION TWELVE

ULTIMATE SUSTENANCE

Deuteronomy 8; 28

SESSION FOCUS

God tested and humbled the Israelites to teach them to depend on Him alone. Jesus shows us our need to humble ourselves and to rely only on Him.

KEY VERSE

He humbled you, causing you to hunger and then feeding you with manna, which neither you nor your fathers had known, to teach you that man does not live on bread alone but on every word that comes from the mouth of the LORD.

DEUTERONOMY 8:3

SESSION AT A GLANCE

Section	60 Min.	90 Min.	What You Will Do
Getting started	10	15	Pray and worship
Main points of the chapter	25	35	Discuss how and why we should depend only on God for sustenance
Application and discussion	15	25	Discuss personal application questions
Looking ahead	5	5	Prepare for next week
Wrapping up	5	10	Close with prayer or song

In 1869, John Muir got a summer job as a shepherd in Tuolumne Meadows in Yosemite, giving him the opportunity to spend lots of time hiking, climbing and studying the mountains, glaciers, plants and animals. He wrote a journal of that summer, later published as *My First Summer in the Sierra*.

STONE SERMONS

On August 9, Muir described Cathedral Peak, one of the outstanding granite spires rising out of the Upper Tuolomne Basin:

> From the top of the divide, and also from the big Tuolumne Meadows, the wonderful mountain called Cathedral Peak is in sight. From every point of view it shows marked individuality. It is a majestic temple of one stone, hewn from the living rock, and adorned with spires and pinnacles in regular cathedral style. The dwarf pines on the roof look like mosses. I hope some time to climb to it to say my prayers and hear the stone sermons.[1]

This is not too different from when the Pharisees tried to hush Jesus' disciples from openly praising him. Nature tells the glory of God, but we need to attune our ears to hear it. A few weeks later, Muir spoke again of Cathedral Peak, issuing his own "church" invitation:

> The Cathedral is said to be about eleven thousand feet above the sea, but the height of the building itself above the level of the ridge it stands on is about fifteen hundred feet. A mile or so to the westward there is a handsome lake, and the glacier-polished granite about it is shining so brightly it is not easy in some places to trace the line between the rock and water, both shining alike. Of this lake with its silvery basin and bits of meadow and groves I have a fine view from the spires; also of Lake Tenaya, Cloud's Rest, and the South Dome of Yosemite, Mt. Starr King, Mt. Hoffman, the Merced peaks, and the vast multitude of snowy fountain peaks extending far north and south along the axis of the range. No feature, however, of all the noble landscape as seen from here seems more wonderful than the Cathedral itself, a temple displaying Nature's best masonry and sermons in stones. How often I have gazed at it from the tops of hills and ridges, and through openings in the forests on my many short excursions, devoutly wondering, admiring, longing! This I may say is the first time I have been at church in California, led here at last, every door graciously opened for the poor lonely worshiper. In our best times everything turns into religion, all the world seems a church and the mountains altars. And lo, here at last in front of the Cathedral is blessed cas-

siope, ringing her thousands of sweet-toned bells, the sweetest church music I ever enjoyed.[2]

Obviously, Muir was able to experience devout worship of God in the natural wonders he explored, and he makes clear that such cathedrals and the sermons one can hear in them are available for all to see and hear. One can't help but wonder if along with the ringing he heard done by Arctic bell-heathers (a plant with bell-shaped flowers), did he also hear the song sung by "all the earth" (Psalm 96:1).

INSPIRATION AND ASPIRATION

Nature inspires us to respond to God's greatness, power and delicacy. We can experience God's glory in nature and, to some extent, be transformed by that experience. But God has also made us morally and spiritually aspirational. We look at how things are, and we want them to be better; we want to strive to meet a higher ideal. So we desire things to be different. We want God to act in us, our relationships, our homes, our communities, our nation, our world—we would like to see things changed, we want things moving on the right, godly track. In short, Christian faith isn't about accepting things just as they are. We want God to intervene. More than that, we *need* God to intervene. And the way we talk to God about what we want is through prayer.

Prayer begins by taking time to stop, coming in to God's presence, sitting down, and spending time listening. Sometimes God's voice is subtle. Sometimes we need a little time down on earth, in the silence, so we can hear what's up in heaven. We don't even have to be in church to be "in church."

Jesus gave us reason to believe that God not only can intervene but also wants to intervene. And Jesus told us exactly how to go about getting our prayers answered when He taught His disciples how to pray and told a story about a persistent friend (see Luke 11:1-12), and when He told the parable about the persistent widow (see Luke 18:1-8).

PRAYER AND PERSISTENCE

Jesus' disciples had noticed that Jesus would very often go off by Himself and pray, that He had a very close relationship with God the Father, and that just about everywhere Jesus went, miracles and changed lives followed.

Finally, one of the disciples asked Jesus to teach the disciples to pray just as John the Baptist had taught his disciples to pray.

THE LORD'S PRAYER

Jesus apparently had been waiting for this moment, so He taught them what we now call the Lord's Prayer:

> Father, hallowed be your name, your kingdom come. Give us each day our daily bread. Forgive us our sins, for we also forgive everyone who sins against us. And lead us not into temptation (Luke 11:2-4; see also Matthew 6:9-13).

Jesus said that we first are to acknowledge that God is our Creator, the Father of us all. Because God is holy ("hallowed"), so is His name. Remember that the third commandment says that we are not to "misuse the name of the LORD your God, for the LORD will not hold anyone guiltless who misuses his name" (Exodus 20:7). The idea is that because of who God is (His character, glory and fame), everyone in the entire world should hold His name in high regard.

Because God's name is holy, we should be disturbed when people use His name in vain or when people make comments that reveal warped ideas about who God is. We should earnestly desire to safeguard God's name.

OLD WEST CHARACTERS

SAM HOUSTON (1793–1863)

Sam Houston was a statesman, politician, solider and first president of the Republic of Texas. The Republic was formed in 1836 when settlers in Texas won a decisive victory against Mexico, who had previously held the territory, at the Battle of San Jacinto. After the state was annexed by the U.S. in 1845—a move that Houston supported—he went into politics and was serving as a senator when the Mexican-American War broke out in 1846. He became governor of Texas in 1859, but was evicted in 1861 for refusing to take an oath of loyalty to the Confederacy. The city of Houston is named after him.

Photo: Courtesy of Special Collections, University of Houston. Public domain

That doesn't mean that God can't take care of His own reputation or that He needs us to defend Him. But because we are His children, we should have a large measure of family loyalty. God bought our loyalty through the cross; that should mean that we want our lives to reflect and respond to that kind of love.

Jesus said that we are to pray for God's kingdom purposes. Notice that the prayer isn't "my kingdom come"; our personal preferences and agendas aren't necessarily God's. There's a sort of built-in correction tape in this part of the prayer. Notice also that this part of the prayer isn't about praying for the end of the world to come. It's about asking God to help us be part of what He's doing in the world on a daily basis: "I want today to count for You, Father. Help me be open to what You are doing and participate with You in that. I want to ask You only for what Your will is for me."

Then, Jesus said, we are to pray for our basic needs. This part of the prayer might seem unnecessary, but at the same time we pray for ourselves, we pray for the benefit of others; and not everyone in the world has their basic needs met every day.

Our asking for our sins to be forgiven comes next. This request is based on our forgiving others for their sins against us. This is one of Jesus' core principles: God loved us first; therefore, we are to love others. God forgave us; therefore, we are to forgive others. If we don't love and forgive others, we haven't really appropriated God's love and forgiveness in our own lives.

Finally, Jesus said that we are to ask God to guide us away from everything that may tempt us to do wrong. This means, though, that we are to try to avoid tempting situations ourselves and that we remove them from our lives. We can pretend that we don't have weaknesses, but our actions will tell us out. We need to be aware of those things or situations that tempt us and then we need to avoid them. To do that, we need God's help and power.

BOLD PERSISTENCE

After Jesus taught His disciples what to pray, He taught them how to pray (see Luke 11:5-13). Jesus first told them about a hypothetical situation: Suppose a friend has a late-night visitor, so at midnight he goes to his neighbor to borrow some bread for the guest. (Hospitality in biblical times was particularly important, so turning away a friend who shows up at your door was not an option.) The neighbor would probably complain about being bothered so late at night, but suppose the friend continues to knock and ask for bread anyway. Finally the friend is rewarded for his persistence (or boldness), and the neighbor gets up and gives him as much bread as he needs.

Notice that the neighbor doesn't give the bread because of their relationship to each other. The neighbor gave him the bread because the friend persisted in asking for it. Then Jesus told His disciples to approach God with the same kind of bold persistence: They were to ask, seek and knock, until the door was opened. Jesus assured His disciples—and that includes us—that if they will keep praying for what they want, God will answer their prayers.

Jesus went on to point out that God, like any good father, will not give us anything that will harm us or that He knows is not good for us (see verses 11-12). In other words, God does not always answer our prayers in the way we want or when we want Him to do so. Persistence may pay off, but so does patience.

Finally, Jesus pointed out that if earthly fathers, who are flawed because of sin, can give (and do give) good gifts to their children, "how much more will your Father in heaven [who is not only good but also perfect!] give the Holy Spirit to those who ask him!" (verse 13). Jesus here implies that the best gift we can receive is being filled with the Holy Spirit, which is what God already wants to give us.

Persistent Pestering

Jesus' parable of the persistent widow is also meant to teach us to pray and never give up praying. A widow asked a judge to give her justice against an enemy. But the judge "neither feared God nor cared about men," so he ignored the widow (Luke 18:2). And he kept ignoring her. Finally, he was so bothered by the widow that he gave her what she asked for just so she would go away.

Jesus pointed out that if a judge who didn't care about God or other people or the difference between right and wrong finally gave the widow justice because of her persistent pestering, how much more God (who certainly cares for people and is just) will do for those who persist in prayer (see Luke 18:6-8).

Remember that in biblical times, widows had a hard time of it, because they had to depend on others to help them and see to their needs. In this story, the widow had only her persistence and being on the side of right (needing justice) to support her. So clearly it was her persistence that finally got her what she wanted.

# REFLECTION QUESTIONS

Read Matthew 14:23 and Mark 1:35. Where did Jesus go to pray?

How is what Jesus did similar to what John Muir did?

Read Job 31:24-28. Although we can go to nature to pray, what are we not to do?

Read Luke 9:28-36 (see also Matthew 17:1-8; Mark 9:2-8). What happened to Jesus when He went to pray on a mountain?

How can prayer transfigure, or change, us?

Although we don't have to be in church to experience "church," why is it important to get together with other believers (see Hebrews 10:25)?

Read 1 Samuel 1:1-20. For what did Hannah keep on praying, and what happened as a result of her persistence (see verses 11,20)?

Session Twelve: Ultimate Sustenance

Read Matthew 6:5-8. Why did Jesus say that some people who pray are hypocrites (see verse 5)?

What advantages are there in being alone when you pray, as Jesus suggested (see verse 6)?

According to verse 7, how long or short should our prayers be?

What characteristics of God are revealed in the Lord's Prayer?

According to Luke 11:2 and 1 John 5:13-14, what is one of the conditions for our prayers to be answered?

Notes
1. John Muir, *My First Summer in the Sierra*, August 9, quoted at "John Muir Writings," *Yosemite Online,* 1997-2011. http://www.yosemite.ca.us/john_muir_writings/my_first_summer_in_the_sierra/chapter_8.html.
2. Ibid., September 7.

APPENDIX A

LEADING A BIBLE STUDY

> Obey your leaders and submit to their authority. They keep watch over you as men who must give an account. Obey them so that their work will be a joy, not a burden, for that would be of no advantage to you.
>
> HEBREWS 13:17

The following are some general guidelines for leaders to follow when using this *SonSeekers* Bible Study with a small group. Note that each of the sessions is designed to be used in either 60-minute or 90-minute meetings (see the overview page for a session outline). Generally, the ideal size for a group is between 10 to 20 people, which is small enough for meaningful fellowship but large enough for dynamic group interaction. It is typically best to stop opening up the group to members after the second session and invite them to join the next study after the 12 weeks are complete.

GROUP DYNAMICS

Getting a group of people actively involved in discussing issues of the Christian life is highly worthwhile. Not only does group interaction help to create interest, stimulate thinking and encourage effective learning, but it is also vital for building quality relationships within the group. Only as people begin to share their thoughts and feelings will they begin to build bonds of friendship and support.

However, some people resist participating in groups that feature interaction—and with good reason. Discussions can, and often do, encounter any number of the following problems:

- Rabbit trails—the group gets off-track, and soon you and the group members are discussing something that doesn't relate in any way to the topic at hand.

- Pooling ignorance—group members express opinions and feelings without having any solid knowledge of the topic.
- Filibuster—a group member talks so much or so often that others are intimidated into non-participation (see the "shrinking violet" description below).
- Discomfort zone—group members believe they are expected to talk about matters that make them feel awkward.
- Shrinking violet—a group member is intimidated into silence.
- Flying fur—opening up for comments from individuals results in disagreements being aired.
- Popularity poll—issues end up being "resolved" by majority opinion rather than on knowledge of the subject.

Granted, some people will prefer to bypass any group participation and get right to the content ("I just want to study the Bible—I don't have time to get to know a bunch of strangers"). However, it is never possible to effectively separate knowledge and love. Information without relationship is sterile, and truth apart from touch will turn to untruth. For this reason, while group interaction may at times seem difficult and even nonproductive, leaders and group members can work together to achieve positive results.

LEADING THE GROUP

The following tips can be helpful in making group interaction a positive learning opportunity for everyone:

- When a question or comment is raised that is off the subject, either suggest that it be dealt with at another time or ask the group if they would prefer to pursue the new issue at that time.

- When someone talks too much, direct a few questions specifically to other people, making sure not to put any shy people on the spot. Talk privately with the "dominator" and ask for cooperation in helping to draw out the quieter group members.

- When someone does not participate verbally, assign a few questions to be discussed in pairs, trios or other small groups, or distribute paper and pencil and invite people to write their answer

Appendix A: Leading a Bible Study

to a specific question or two. Then invite several people (including the quiet ones) to read what they wrote.

- If someone asks a question that you don't know how to answer, admit it and move on. If the question calls for insight about personal experience, invite group members to comment. If the question requires specialized knowledge, offer to look for an answer before the next session (make sure to follow up the next session).

- When group members disagree with you or each other, remind them that it is possible to disagree without becoming disagreeable. To help clarify the issues while maintaining a climate of mutual acceptance, encourage those on opposite sides to restate what they have heard the other person(s) saying about the issue. Then invite each side to evaluate how accurately they feel their position was presented. Ask group members to identify as many points as possible related to the topic on which both sides agree, and then lead the group in examining other Scriptures related to the topic, looking for common ground that they can all accept.

- Finally, urge group members to keep an open heart and mind and a willingness to continue loving one another while learning more about the topic at hand.

If the disagreement involves an issue on which your church has stated a position, be sure that stance is clearly and positively presented. This should be done not to squelch dissent but to ensure there is no confusion over where your church stands.

APPENDIX B

JOINING GOD'S FAMILY

If we confess our sins, he is faithful and just and will forgive us our sins and purify us from all unrighteousness.

1 JOHN 1:9

Jesus is truly always with you, and He wants you to be a member of His family. So, if you haven't yet commited your life to Christ, why not make that decision today? Simply read through and follow the steps below. If you want to help a friend, a relative or a student of any age become a member of God's family, use the material presented here as a guide to help a new believer declare his or her faith.[1]

INTRODUCTION

In the Old Testament, God promised to send a Messiah, or Savior, to His people. The Messiah would save God's people from their sins, from the wrong things everyone has done. The people in Old Testament times knew about the promise of a Savior and looked for Him.

In the New Testament, God's promise came true! The Savior was born in Bethlehem, just where God had promised (see Micah 5:2). Jesus Christ was born, grew up and died for our sins.

God's Word always comes true. You can trust God's faithfulness, for He made it possible for you to become a member of His family. Just read through the five easy steps given here.

STEP 1: GOD LOVES YOU

The Bible says in 1 John 4:8 that "God is love." He loves you very much. He loves you because He made you and He is concerned about you and your life today.

STEP 2: YOU HAVE SINNED

The Bible also says that you and all other people have sinned. In Romans 3:23 we read, "For all have sinned and fall short of the glory of God."

We have all done wrong, and our sins keep us from being friends with God. As you read in the books of the Old Testament, sin always leads to trouble. Because you are a sinner, your sin will cause much trouble in your life. Romans 6:23 tells how bad this trouble will ultimately be: "The wages of sin is death."

God does not want you to ruin your life with sin. It makes Him sad when you sin and spoil your happiness and the happiness of other people. Because of sin, you cannot enjoy God's loving presence in your life, and you can't live with God in heaven. Not one of us by even our very best efforts is able to remove sin from our lives or to earn God's forgiveness.

In the beginning of the Bible is the story of Adam and Eve, the first two people. Adam and Eve lived happily with God until they disobeyed Him. That was the first sin. One of the results of that sin was that Adam and Eve were separated from God, thereby robbing life of its greatest joy and ultimately bringing the penalty of death on themselves. All of us sin, so someday each of us will die, too.

However, the Bible is clear that there is another life after we die. The Bible is also clear that sin will continue to separate people from God's love forever. Because everybody has sinned, how does anybody get to go to heaven?

STEP 3: GOD PAID THE PRICE

The Bible says in Romans 6:23, "The wages of sin is death, but the gift of God is eternal life in Christ Jesus our Lord." The result of sin is death. However, because God loves you so much, He offers eternal life as a free gift. You cannot work hard enough to earn eternal life. All you can do is accept it as a gift.

God gave His only Son to die for you on the cross. The Bible says in 1 Corinthians 15:3, "Christ died for our sins according to the Scriptures." Because Jesus was the perfect man (without sin) He accepted the results of sin (death) in your place. The Bible says in 1 John 4:14, "The Father has sent his Son to be the Savior of the world."

STEP 4: GOD WILL FORGIVE YOU

If you admit that you have sinned and believe that God gave His only Son to die in your place, God will forgive you and make you clean from all sin.

Tell God that you know you are a sinner.

Tell God that you believe Jesus Christ is the only way to have your sins forgiven.

Tell God that you want to learn to love and follow Christ in every area of your life.

Tell God that He is great and wonderful.

It is easy to talk to God. Jesus taught us to talk to Him as we would to a loving Father. He is ready to listen. What you are going to tell Him is something He has been waiting to hear.

If you believe and have told God you believe, you are now a child of God! God has forgiven all your sins. You are a Christian. And that makes you a member of God's family.

God has made everything right between you and Him. He has forgiven you and He looks on you as if you had never sinned!

STEP 5: YOU CAN LIVE AS GOD'S CHILD

The Bible says in John 1:12, "Yet to all who did receive him, to those who believed in his name, he gave the right to become children of God." As a child of God, you receive God's gift of everlasting life. God is with you now and forever. Now that you are a member of God's family, God wants you to live as His child.

You Can Talk to God

Because God is your heavenly Father, He wants you to talk to Him in prayer. You can tell God how you feel, thank Him for His gifts to you and ask Him to help you obey and follow Him.

You can also talk to God when you sin. Ask God to forgive you and He will. The Bible says in 1 John 1:9, "If we confess our sins, he is faithful and just and will forgive us our sins and purify us from all unrighteousness." God will forgive you and help you do what He says.

You Can Read God's Word

God gave us His Word so that everyone can read about Him and His great love. Find out more about God by reading about Him in *your* Bible. As you read God's Word, you will stay close to Him. You'll get to know Him better and better, and He will help you to always do what is right. The Bible says, "I have hidden your word in my heart that I might not sin against you" (Psalm 119:11).

You Can Obey God

Your heavenly Father wants you to obey Him. He tells you in His Word how you should live. Jesus summed up God's law with two commandments (see Matthew 22:37-40):

1. "Love the Lord your God with all your heart and with all your soul and with all your mind" (Matthew 22:37).
2. "Love your neighbor as yourself" (Matthew 22: 39).

God wants you to be an expression of His love in the world.

You Can Tell Others About Jesus

Jesus said in Acts 1:8, "You will be my witnesses." Jesus was talking to His disciples before He went back to His Father. Even though Jesus was talking to His disciples, He was saying these words to you, too. You can be a witness by telling others about Jesus and how His love has helped you. Ask God to give you opportunities each day to tell about—and to show—God's love.

Note
1. The following is taken from Dr. Henrietta C. Mears, *What the Bible Is All About* (Ventura, CA: Regal, 2011), pp. 783-786.

ALSO AVAILABLE FROM
GOSPEL LIGHT

Jesus Is with Me
Uncommon Youth Elective
ISBN 978-0-8307-6524-9
ISBN 0-8307-6524-7

Facing the uncertainties of life—school, relationships, money, the future—can be daunting for most teenagers. They may feel like a cowboy without a horse . . . in the middle of nowhere! With *Jesus Is with Me*, from the *Uncommon* series of student resources, you can help your young people find encouragement to meet these challenges head-on. The examples of Moses and Joseph will show your teens and tweens that Jesus is with them no matter what life throws at them. Twelve sessions of kid-friendly activities and exercises will introduce your group members to God's ultimate plan to redeem, love, care and provide for them through Jesus. Equip them to strike out on the adventure of life with Jesus at their side. *Jesus Is with Me* is specially designed to be used alongside Gospel Light's *SonWest Roundup* VBS program or as a stand-alone group Bible study. You choose! Includes download reproducible student handouts for every session.

Available at Bookstores Everywhere!
Go to www.regalbooks.com to learn more about your favorite Regal books and authors. Visit us online today!

God's Word for Your World™
www.regalbooks.com

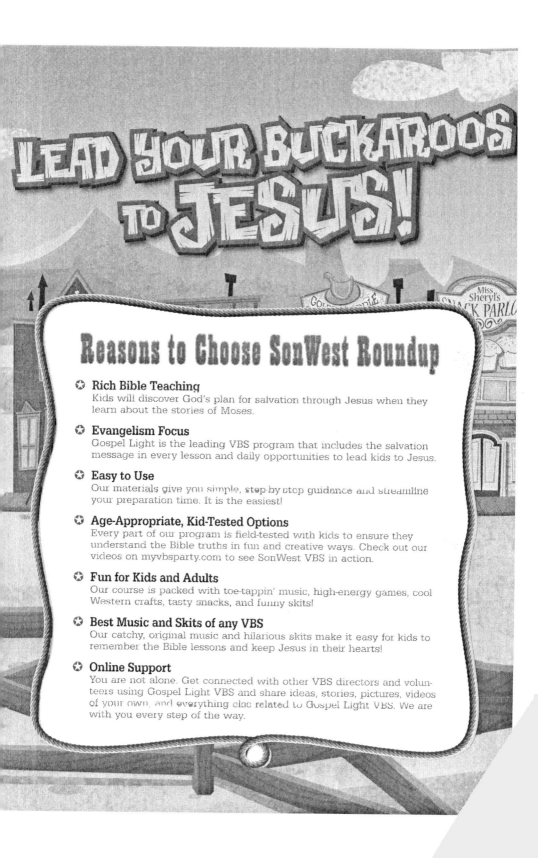

Lead Your Buckaroos to Jesus!

Reasons to Choose SonWest Roundup

- **Rich Bible Teaching**
  Kids will discover God's plan for salvation through Jesus when they learn about the stories of Moses.

- **Evangelism Focus**
  Gospel Light is the leading VBS program that includes the salvation message in every lesson and daily opportunities to lead kids to Jesus.

- **Easy to Use**
  Our materials give you simple, step-by-step guidance and streamline your preparation time. It is the easiest!

- **Age-Appropriate, Kid-Tested Options**
  Every part of our program is field-tested with kids to ensure they understand the Bible truths in fun and creative ways. Check out our videos on myvbsparty.com to see SonWest VBS in action.

- **Fun for Kids and Adults**
  Our course is packed with toe-tappin' music, high-energy games, cool Western crafts, tasty snacks, and funny skits!

- **Best Music and Skits of any VBS**
  Our catchy, original music and hilarious skits make it easy for kids to remember the Bible lessons and keep Jesus in their hearts!

- **Online Support**
  You are not alone. Get connected with other VBS directors and volunteers using Gospel Light VBS and share ideas, stories, pictures, videos of your own, and everything else related to Gospel Light VBS. We are with you every step of the way.

WHAT THE BIBLE IS ALL ABOUT®
BIBLE STUDY SERIES

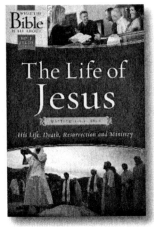

THE LIFE OF JESUS
Matthew–John
ISBN 978-0-8307-5946-0

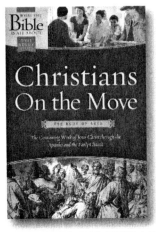

CHRISTIANS ON THE MOVE
The Book of Acts
ISBN 978-0-8307-6130-2

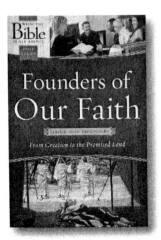

FOUNDERS OF OUR FAITH
Genesis–Deuteronomy
ISBN 978-0-8307-5948-4

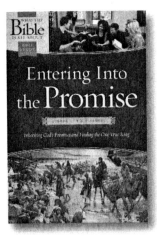

ENTERING INTO THE PROMISE
Joshua–1 & 2 Samuel
ISBN 978-0-8307-6220-0

the Bible Come Alive Like Never Before!

scover *What the Bible Is All About®*
it us today at www.gospellight.com